Life Changing Journey

750 Inspirational Quotes

SERIES I

"Unveiling Wisdom: Inspiring Quotes to Spark Your Life. A Treasury of Inspiration for Cultivating Positivity on Life, Love, Nature, and More."

SHREE SHAMBAV

Life Changing Journey – Series I
750 Inspirational Quotes
Shree Shambav

Published by Shree Shambav, Tamil Nadu, India

All Rights Reserved
First Edition, 2024
Second Edition 2025
Copyright © 2025, Muniswamy Rajakumar

All rights reserved. No part of this publication may be reproduced, distributed, or transmitted in any form or by any means, including photocopying, recording, or other electronic or mechanical methods, without the author's prior written permission. It is illegal to copy this book, post it to a website, or distribute it by any other means without permission.

The request for permission should be addressed to the author.

ISBN: 978-93-343-2491-4

Email:shreeshambav@gmail.com

Web:www.shambav.org

DEDICATION

"Isavasyam idam sarvam yat kim ca jagatyam jagat, tena tyaktena bhunjitha, ma gridhah kasyasvid dhanam"

To the Almighty,

the Divine Masters,

the family who listens,

and my parents who see –

your presence shapes the pages of my life's journey.

"Isavasyam idam sarvam yat kim ca jagatyam jagat"

Meaning: "God encompasses everything you perceive, see, or touch with your sense organs."

DISCLAIMER

This book, *"Life-Changing Journey - Inspirational Quotes: Series I,"* is a heartfelt compilation of personal reflections and insights born from the author's journey of understanding life and the natural world. Each inspirational quote is a subjective truth—a distillation of experience and thought—meant to serve as a mirror for readers to explore their own perspectives and uncover meaning through the lens of their unique experiences.

The intention behind this book is to share a message imbued with compassion, love, and care. It is designed to inspire readers on their personal journeys and guide them toward discovering the deeper realities of life. This is not a prescriptive manual but an invitation to pause, reflect, and engage with life's profound yet simple truths.

It's important to acknowledge that neither the content nor the sequence of the quotes is intended to cause harm, discomfort, or conflict with the reader's personal beliefs. Should any part of the book feel unsettling or contradictory to one's convictions, it is purely coincidental and never intentional.

The journey through these quotes is one of openness and fluidity, free from rigid interpretations or dogmatic assertions. The content reflects the author's personal perspective and is humbly offered as a source of inspiration and gentle guidance. Readers are invited to engage with the material at their own pace, to reflect deeply, and to adapt the wisdom within to align with their inner truths and life experiences.

Above all, this book aspires to spark joy, nurture connection, and encourage purposeful living. It gently beckons readers to cultivate a life rooted in compassion, integrity, and intentionality while embracing the beauty of each moment with grace and mindfulness. May the words within these pages illuminate your path as you embark on a transformative journey of self-discovery, growth, and renewal. The journey is uniquely yours, and it is an honour for the author to accompany you, even if only in spirit, as you navigate the unfolding of your life.

With this understanding, readers are encouraged to approach the book with an open mind and heart, recognising that its wisdom is offered not as universal truth but as a collection of insights shaped by the author's personal experiences. You are invited to absorb what resonates, reinterpret what feels unfamiliar, and find your own meaning within these words.

Ultimately, the author's deepest wish is that these reflections serve as a beacon of hope, a source of motivation, and a catalyst for positivity as you embark on your life-changing journey. May this book inspire you to walk your path with courage, grace, and an unwavering belief in the beauty of life's unfolding.

Note - If any part of the book, in any sequence, hurts the reader's sentiments, it would be just out of a sheer accident, not intentional

Divine

"When the river meets the ocean, it recognises that it was the ocean from the beginning till the end. Likewise, when a self-surrender to the higher self occurs, the self becomes the 'Divine'."

– Shree Shambav

EPIGRAM

In the quiet of a single thought lies the power to awaken a thousand hearts.
In each word, a mirror; in each pause, a path.
This journey is not to escape life, but to meet it fully—soul to soul.

– Shree Shambav

Life Changing Journey

750 Plus Inspirational Quotes

Shree Shambav

Shree Shambav is a 41x best-selling author renowned for his transformative works in personal development and spiritual growth.

Dear Cherished Readers

Dear Cherished Readers,

As I embark on this new literary voyage, my heart swells with profound gratitude and an overwhelming sense of connection. With deep emotion, I extend my heartfelt appreciation to each of you who has joined me on this journey.

With sincere warmth, I invite you to revisit the steps we have taken together through the pages of my earlier works. Our odyssey began with "Journey of Soul - Karma," a book that marked my first foray into the world of words and a testament to the raw passion that ignited my writing adventure.

The subsequent chapters of our shared narrative unfolded through the enchanting tapestry of the "Twenty + One" series. Each page turned was a brushstroke on the canvas of our imaginations, painting vivid stories that I hoped would resonate deeply within your hearts.

And how can I forget the transformative journey we embarked on with the "Life Changing Journey - Inspirational Quotes Series." Day by day, quote by quote, we delved into reflections that uplifted, inspired, and sought to bring a glimpse of light to our souls.

The release of "Death - Light of Life and the Shadow of Death" promises to shed new light on the timeless mystery of death.

The **Optimum Python Series** is a comprehensive guide designed to empower readers at every stage of their programming journey. It begins with *Series I: Ultimate Guide for Beginners*, which lays a strong foundation in Python, making it accessible and engaging for newcomers. *Series II: Exploring Data Structures and Algorithms* takes the next step, offering a deep dive into core computer science principles that enhance problem-solving skills and coding efficiency. Building on this, *Series III: Python Power for Data Science* introduces powerful libraries such as NumPy, Pandas, Matplotlib, and Scikit-learn, guiding readers through data manipulation, visualisation, and foundational machine learning techniques. Finally, *Series IV: Unleashing the Potential of Data Science with Machine Learning Techniques* explores advanced machine learning models and real-world applications, enabling readers to harness the full potential of data-driven insights. Whether you're just starting out or looking to master sophisticated tools and strategies, this series is your roadmap to Python proficiency and beyond.

Shree Shambav expands his artistic repertoire with *"Whispers of Eternity: 150 Plus - A Symphony of Soulful Verses,"* a heartfelt exploration of the human experience. Alongside this, his *"Whispers of the Soul: A Journey Through Haiku"* distils profound insights into poignant verses. Together, these works showcase his versatility and mastery of soulful expression, inviting readers on a journey of self-discovery. Through his poetry, he weaves a rich tapestry of emotion that resonates deeply with the heart.

LIFE CHANGING JOURNEY

Shree Shambav's latest works—*Learn to Love Yourself: A Journey of Discovering Inner Beauty and Strength Through 10 Transformative Rules, The Power of Letting Go: Embrace Freedom and Happiness, A Journey of Lasting Peace*—are true treasures of self-discovery, *The Entitlement Trap: Get Over It, Get On, Whispers of a Dying Soul: Unspoken Regrets and Unlived Dreams, Whispers of Silence - Unlocking Inner Power through Stillness, The Power of Words: Transforming Speech, Transforming Lives, The Art of Intentional Living: Minimalism for a Life of Purpose, Awakening the Infinite: The Power of Consciousness in Transforming Life, Beyond the Veil: A Journey Through Life After Death* series, *Bonds Beyond Blood - Where love builds bridges, and bonds defy blood., A Journey into Spiritual Maturity - 12 Golden Rules for Inner Transformation, The Seeker's Gold: Unlocking Life's Greatest Treasure* and *The Power of Manifestation - Unlocking The Path From Thought To Reality.*

In addition to these works, Shree Shambav has recently ventured into astrology with the release of Astrology Unveiled – Foundations of Ancient Wisdom Series I to VIII, expanding into the realm of metaphysics. These books explore the foundational principles of Vedic astrology, offering readers a rich and practical understanding of this ancient wisdom.

Your unwavering support, enthusiasm to immerse yourself in my writings, and readiness to embark on these journeys with me have been my greatest sources of inspiration. Your input has been a beacon guiding me through the creation process, moulding these stories into containers of passion, emotion, knowledge, and resonance.

As I unveil this new narrative before you, know that your presence, insights, and shared moments have been my companions. The path we have walked together is etched in the annals of my creative evolution, and it's an honour beyond words to have you by my side once more.

Here's to the readers who have illuminated my path with their presence, who have embraced my stories with open hearts, and who have woven themselves into the very fabric of my literary world. Our journey has been a symbiotic dance of writer and reader, a harmony of souls brought together by the magic of storytelling.

With a heart brimming with appreciation and eyes glistening with anticipation, I extend my deepest gratitude for your unwavering support. Thank you for the memories, the shared emotions, and the countless hours spent in the worlds we've crafted together. As we step into this new adventure, let's continue to explore, feel, and discover the boundless horizons that words can unveil.

Warmly,

Shree Shambav

LIFE CHANGING JOURNEY

Suggested Reads

FROM BEST-SELLING AUTHOR

Endorsements

"Life Changing Journey – Inspirational Quotes Series I is more than a book—it is a soulful companion for anyone seeking meaning, strength, and clarity in life's unfolding journey. Shree Shambav masterfully weaves timeless wisdom with everyday truths, offering reflections that gently awaken the heart and uplift the spirit. Each quote is a seed of insight—simple yet profound, comforting yet thought-provoking. Whether you are navigating change, embracing growth, or yearning for inner peace, this book offers the kind of gentle guidance that lingers long after the page is turned. A must-have for every seeker's shelf."

- Akshaya Rajesh (IT Consultant)

.

About the Author

Shree Shambav is an internationally acclaimed, best-selling author, inspirational speaker, artist, philanthropist, life coach, and entrepreneur. A world record holder, his deep passion for music led him to create soul-stirring albums, drawing inspiration from his celebrated poetry collection, Whispers of Eternity. His profound insights have sparked deep personal transformations, guiding countless individuals toward self-discovery, purposeful living, and authenticity.

With an extraordinary ability to unlock human potential, Shree empowers individuals to break through limitations and embrace their highest selves. His writings, lectures, and compassionate guidance continue to uplift lives, fostering resilience, mindfulness, and personal growth.

Shree Shambav is a 41x best-selling author celebrated for his profound contributions to personal development and spiritual growth.

Shree Shambav's literary journey took flight with the celebrated Journey of Soul - Karma, where he delved into the depths of human experience to unveil profound insights. Garnering recognition through multiple literature awards, his repertoire includes esteemed works, such as the Twenty + One Series and the enlightening Life Changing Journey series.

As a distinguished alumnus of the Indian Institute of Management and the National Institute of Technology, Shree Shambav brings a wealth of corporate acumen from his tenure in multinational corporations. His most recent publications, including Unveiling the Enigma, Death - Light of Life and the Shadow of Death and Optimum - Python Series I, Series II, Series III and Series IV, demonstrate his mastery of both the literary and technical spheres.

Shree Shambav expands his artistic repertoire with *"Whispers of Eternity: 150 Plus - A Symphony of Soulful Verses,"* a heartfelt exploration of the human experience. Alongside this, his *"Whispers of the Soul: A Journey Through Haiku"* distils profound insights into poignant verses. Together, these works showcase his versatility and mastery of soulful expression, inviting readers on a journey of self-discovery. Through his poetry, he weaves a rich tapestry of emotion that resonates deeply with the heart.

Shree Shambav's latest works—*Learn to Love Yourself: A Journey of Discovering Inner Beauty and Strength Through 10 Transformative Rules, The Power of Letting Go: Embrace Freedom and Happiness, A*

LIFE CHANGING JOURNEY

Journey of Lasting Peace—are true treasures of self-discovery, The Entitlement Trap: Get Over It, Get On, Whispers of a Dying Soul: Unspoken Regrets and Unlived Dreams, Whispers of Silence - Unlocking Inner Power through Stillness, The Power of Words: Transforming Speech, Transforming Lives, The Art of Intentional Living: Minimalism for a Life of Purpose, Awakening the Infinite:The Power of Consciousness in Transforming Life, Beyond the Veil: A Journey Through Life After Death series, Bonds Beyond Blood - Where love builds bridges, and bonds defy blood., A Journey into Spiritual Maturity - 12 Golden Rules for Inner Transformation, The Seeker's Gold: Unlocking Life's Greatest Treasure and The Power of Manifestation - Unlocking The Path From Thought To Reality.

In addition to these works, Shree Shambav has recently ventured into astrology with the release of Astrology Unveiled – Foundations of Ancient Wisdom Series I to VIII, expanding into the realm of metaphysics. These books explore the foundational principles of Vedic astrology, offering readers a rich and practical understanding of this ancient wisdom.

Shree Shambav established the Ayur Rakshita Foundation, which is dedicated to promoting boundless growth, universal fraternity, and environmental protection. The charity helps diverse communities while working for societal progress.

To learn more about Shree Shambav and his works, visit his website at www.shambav.org. For information about the Ayur Rakshita Foundation and its initiatives, visit www.shambav-ayurrakshita.org.

Let's Follow him on Social Media: **@shreeshambav**

Main: https://linktr.ee/shreeshambav

SHREE SHAMBAV

Website: https://www.shambav.org/

LinkedIn: https://www.linkedin.com/in/shreeshambav/

Blog: https://blog.shambav.org/

Instagram: https://www.instagram.com/shreeshambav/

YouTube: https://www.youtube.com/@shreeshambav

Amazon: https://www.amazon.com/author/shreeshambav

Goodreads: https://www.goodreads.com/author/show/22367436.Shree_Shambav

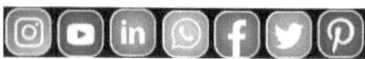

FOREWORD

Shree Shambav is an alumnus of the IIM and the NIT. He has had a distinguished career in the corporate world. In the corporate world, resources alone do not decide the outcomes, and just the outcomes do not judge the longevity of business and commerce. Business and commerce can thrive only when they are hinged on the culture created from within. And, when we talk of culture, whether in businesses or civil societies, our understanding of people's expectations comes to the fore. Therefore, the foremost principle of life, i.e., selflessness, gets emblazoned on whatever it is worth.

Shree Shambav Ayur Rakshita Foundation (www.shambav-ayurrakshita.org), founded by him, aids all communities towards fostering limitless growth, universal brotherhood and self-realisation of the undying need to protect nature, its munificence and its liberality.

Famous people have framed famous quotations. They are inspiring, but to frame quotations directly related to our simple lives is no small matter. For example, on a warm and sultry day, when a breeze brushes past you, you feel the sensation but cannot see it, and thus the quote, "The most beautiful things are unseen but can be felt."

A person on the verge of giving up is trudging along a deserted street, aimless and desperate. He finds a slogan on a defaced wall. It reads, "Giving up is easier; holding oneself up is wiser." Such a simple saying or quote can awaken any person from a stupor and may promise a new lease of life. Thus, the achievements of great people can be weighed by the quintessential power of their quotes.

Colonel N Sailendra Rao (Retired)

PREFACE

Life is a symphony, and each moment plays its own note in the grand orchestration of existence. Within this ever-evolving melody, words hold a sacred and timeless power—they awaken dormant truths, soothe invisible wounds, and ignite the spirit with renewed hope. *Life Changing Journey – Inspirational Quotes Series* by Shree Shambav is far more than a collection of phrases; it is a soulful companion, a quiet guide, and a radiant beacon for those traversing the intricate and often uncertain pathways of life.

This book was conceived in the stillness where true inspiration breathes—in those sacred pauses when the noise of the world recedes, and the voice of the soul begins to rise. Each quote is a drop of distilled wisdom, a mirror reflecting universal truths through the lens of simplicity and depth. These words echo the shared heartbeat of human experience, inviting the reader into a contemplative space where healing, clarity, and transformation quietly unfold.

Structured with intention and grace, each chapter explores a unique dimension of the human spirit. They illuminate the courage it takes to embrace change, the resilience needed to pursue dreams, and the wisdom found in the face of adversity. They explore the tenderness of love, the beauty of authentic self-acceptance, and the quiet power that lies dormant within us all. These pages whisper of joy rooted in simplicity, gratitude awakened by mindfulness, and the sacred interconnectedness we share with nature, the cosmos, and one another.

This book is a living tapestry of timeless insights—threads of light woven to transcend circumstance and awaken the soul. It invites you to pause, reflect, and reconnect with the deeper wisdom that resides within. Whether you are weathering personal storms, seeking the spark to chase your aspirations, or longing for inner stillness and peace, the quotes within offer not just inspiration but companionship for the road ahead. A trusted confidant through life's journey, this collection invites you to discover the power of presence, purpose, and the quiet miracles waiting in every moment.

Life Changing Journey – Inspirational Quotes Series I beautifully explores the many dimensions of human experience. Through themes like Karma, Divinity, True Love, and Cosmic Principles, it offers deep reflections on life, purpose, and wisdom. Each chapter invites the reader to pause, reflect, and grow from within.

In Series II, "Life Changing Journey – Inspirational Quotes Series II", gracefully weaves together a rich tapestry of themes that reflect the many layers of the human experience. This collection explores the journey of Discovering Self and nurturing Dreams and Aspirations, while embracing life's inevitable transitions through Embracing Change and Embracing Imperfections. It offers strength through Finding Inner Strength, and serenity through Gratitude and Mindfulness. The series uplifts with Inspiration and Motivation, imparts resilience through Lessons from

Adversity, and celebrates the depth of Love and Relationships. It honours the harmony found in Nature's Symphony and encourages the pursuit of purpose in Pursuing Your Dreams. With reflections on Serenity and Balance, Shades of Existence, and Success and Achievement, it invites readers to find meaning in The Beauty of Simplicity and The Power of Kindness. The journey culminates in soulful reflections such as Whispers of the Divine and timeless Wisdom from the Ages, offering profound insight and guidance for every step of life's path."

Series III, themes like *"Embracing Change," "Discovering Self," "Dreams and Aspirations," "Embracing Imperfections," "Finding Inner Strength,"* and *"Gratitude and Mindfulness"* invite you to reflect on identity, purpose, and the pursuit of your passions.

Series IV delves deeper into *"Inspiration and Motivation," "Lessons from Adversity," "Love and Relationships," "Nature's Symphony," "Pursuing Your Dreams,"* and *"Serenity and Balance"*— nurturing connections, fostering resilience, and celebrating life's harmony.

Series V culminates in the profound, with themes like *"Shades of Existence," "Success and Achievement," "The Beauty of Simplicity," "The Power of Kindness,"* and *"Wisdom from the Ages."* These chapters remind us to cherish the beauty in life's simplest moments and draw strength from timeless truths.

Series VI culminates in a journey of inner stillness and soulful reflection, exploring themes such as *"Embracing Change," "Love and Relationships," "Serenity and Balance," "Shades of Existence,"* and *"Whispers of the Divine."* Each chapter gently invites us to slow down, to find meaning in silence, and to recognise the sacred in everyday life. They are reminders that life's simplest moments often carry the most profound truths and that true strength arises when we listen deeply—to others, to nature, and to our hearts.

Series VII deepens this introspection, guiding us through themes like *"Discovering the Self," "Finding Inner Strength," "Lessons from Adversity," "The Power of Kindness,"* and *"Wisdom from the Ages."*

Series VIII invites readers on a deeper path of introspection, embracing themes like change, imperfections, and inner strength.

Rooted in mindfulness, gratitude, and inspiration, it nurtures quiet resilience and clarity.

Through nature's rhythms and life's simple truths, it gently reminds us that lasting transformation begins within.

These chapters serve as lanterns on the path of growth—illuminating how hardship refines us, how kindness transforms, and how the wisdom of those who walked before us still echoes with relevance today. They remind us that every challenge holds a lesson, and every moment offers a choice to awaken.

Shree Shambav's words transcend the mundane, touching the sacred essence of life. They serve as gentle reminders of our shared humanity, encouraging us to embrace imperfections and live authentically. Each quote is a spark—a catalyst for growth and self-discovery, illuminating the path through life's trials and triumphs.

LIFE CHANGING JOURNEY

As you turn these pages, may you find not just words but a profound connection to your inner self and the world around you. Let this collection be a sanctuary of wisdom, a reservoir of courage, and a wellspring of inspiration, empowering you to embrace life with an open heart and an awakened soul.

Welcome to the *"Life Changing Journey - Inspirational Quotes Series."* May this book inspire you to live boldly, love deeply, and discover the boundless joy within your own journey.

Let the journey unfold.

With gratitude and encouragement,

Shree Shambav

INTRODUCTION

In a world that moves with relentless speed—filled with expectations, responsibilities, and constant noise—it's easy to drift away from what truly matters. We chase deadlines, strive for perfection, and race from one task to another, yet deep within, many of us yearn for something more. Something that nourishes the soul, anchors us in truth, and rekindles our sense of wonder.

That quiet yearning—the whisper beneath the rush—is the seed from which the *Life Changing Journey – Inspirational Quotes Series* was born. This book is not merely a collection of quotes; it is an invitation. A gentle call to pause, to reflect, and to remember the deeper wisdom that surrounds us and lives within us.

Words, when offered with sincerity and soul, have the power to change the course of a day—or a life. A single phrase, encountered at the right moment, can offer clarity in chaos, light in darkness, or courage in fear. This collection was curated with that transformative potential in mind. Each quote is a distillation of timeless truths, crafted to awaken the strength, hope, and resilience that already dwell within you.

Life Changing Journey – Inspirational Quotes Series I takes readers on a soulful exploration of the human experience, weaving together powerful themes such as Cosmic Life Principles, Divinity, Karma, and the Treasure of Learning. Each section offers reflections that gently guide the heart and mind toward deeper awareness, purpose, and wisdom. Whether exploring the truths of Maya (Illusion), the grounding force of Values and Beliefs, or the beauty of looking deeply into nature, this series provides a space for contemplation and connection with life's deeper meanings.

From understanding True Love and True Wisdom to gaining new Views and Perspectives, each quote serves as a stepping stone toward personal transformation. The series encourages readers to see beyond the veil of everyday distractions and reconnect with the essence of who they are. Ideal for moments of stillness or daily reflection, these carefully curated themes resonate with seekers of inner growth, clarity, and peace.

These are not just themes—they are stepping stones for transformation. Each one invites you to see life not merely as a series of events but as a sacred unfolding of who you truly are. They gently guide you to find beauty in imperfection, strength in stillness, and clarity in silence.

This book is not meant to be consumed in one sitting. It is meant to be lived with. Revisited. Rediscovered. Like a trusted friend, it will meet you where you are—whether you are standing at a crossroads, moving through a challenge, or celebrating a quiet victory. In moments of doubt, may these words bring assurance. In times of transition, may they offer direction. And in moments of joy, may they deepen your gratitude.

In an age when the world constantly pulls us outward, this book gently invites you inward—to reconnect with your inner compass, to realign with your truth, and to remember that the answers you seek often rise from stillness.

As you turn its pages, I hope you find more than inspiration. I hope you find a connection. With yourself. With others. And with the wonder that lives quietly in each moment. May these quotes serve not only as reflections of truth, but as a light to illuminate your unique path.

This is your journey. Your sacred unfolding. May these words give you the courage to live it fully, authentically, and with grace.

With love and gratitude,

Shree Shambav

PROLOGUE

The Soul's Silent Compass

There are chapters in life when words become more than just language—they become lifelines. In moments of uncertainty, silence, or awakening, a single sentence can become a lantern in the dark, a whisper of strength, or a mirror reflecting a truth we had long forgotten. Life Changing Journey – Inspirational Quotes Series I was born from such moments—crafted not as a collection of borrowed wisdom, but as a heartfelt offering for those walking the winding path of life with open hearts and seeking minds.

This book is a quiet sanctuary—an invitation to pause, to feel, and to reflect. The themes within are not abstract ideas; they are lived experiences. Karma, Divinity, True Wisdom, and Maya (Illusion) are not just philosophical terms, but inner landscapes we all traverse. Each quote is a distillation of universal truths, drawn from the wellspring of ancient insight and timeless observation. They speak of love not just as emotion, but as essence; of learning not just as education, but as evolution; of nature not just as beauty, but as a teacher and guide.

In a world that often rushes us past the soul's whispers, this series invites you to slow down and listen. To reconnect with the voice within. To see life not through the lens of routine, but through the eyes of wonder, awareness, and grace.

Whether you are healing from grief, stepping into growth, seeking clarity, or simply looking for light in the everyday—may these words meet you where you are, and gently guide you to where your spirit longs to be.

Let this be more than a book. Let it be a companion on your life's most sacred journey: the journey inward.

Welcome to the journey.— *Shree Shambav*

CONTENTS

DEDICATION iii
DISCLAIMER v
Divine vii
EPIGRAM ix
Dear Cherished Readers xiii
Suggested Reads xvii
Endorsements xix
About the Author xxi
FOREWORD xxv
PREFACE xxvii
INTRODUCTION xxxiii
PROLOGUE xxxvii
Cosmic Life Principle 1
   Navigating Life's Transformations 1
Divinity 19
   Overcoming Obstacles 19
Karma 43
   Reflections on Identity and Purpose 43
Learning is Treasure 55
   Nurturing Connections 55
Life Insights 75
   Empowering the Mind and Spirit 75
Life Values and Beliefs 99

Embracing Self-Acceptance	99
Look Deep into Nature!	115
Finding Joy in the Present	115
Maya or Illusion	133
Fuelling the Soul	133
See Beyond the Veil	147
Dreams and Aspirations	147
To Achieve in Life	167
Turning Challenges into Growth	167
True Love	191
Spreading Compassion and Love	191
True Wisdom	209
Timeless Insights for Life	209
View and Perspective	233
Cultivating Inner Peace	233
Life is Priceless	251
Life Coach and Philanthropist	255
TESTIMONIALS	257
ACKNOWLEDGEMENTS	265

Cosmic Life Principle
Navigating Life's Transformations

"In the ebb and flow of life's transformations, we discover the strength to weather storms and the grace to embrace new horizons."

- Shree Shambav

A Circle of Becoming

"Each person around the fire held a mirror. Each mirror reflected a different light."

A simple sleep

"Death is nothing more than slumber. Death is nothing more than sleep, just as a man sleeps and wakes up."

Awakening the Inner World

"True transformation begins not in changing the outside, but in awakening the vast, silent universe within—where the soul's wisdom quietly shapes the reality beyond."

Bliss

"When the spirit within him withdraws, as per cosmic law, the physical body disintegrates and dissolves into a cosmic reservoir, and the Prana, or life breath current, combines with the cosmic life principle."

Connection

"There is always a law of connection; we just have to be cognizant of it and tune into it."

Death

"Men all pass away. However, not all men live."

Devotion Moves the Universe

"The universe listens to your vibration, but it moves for your devotion."

Devotion in Small Things

"When she arranged flowers for the altar, it wasn't routine—it was prayer through petals."

Does anything perish?

"Nothing perishes... nothing dies."

Embers and Eyes

"The fire outside may fade, but the fire we met in each other's eyes will not."

Embers of the Soul

"A single ember of faith, buried beneath ashes of loss, can reignite the entire light of your being."

Flawless

"Even the tiniest creatures have the power to deepen your faith and broaden your horizons. A sprout that sprouts from the ground can teach you something valuable. Not only does his work offer us wisdom but also love, passion, hope, and patience. He is flawless, and everything he creates reflects that."

Flicker of the Divine

"Every act of devotion, even one small light, is the soul remembering its divine nature."

From Healing to Offering

"What we receive in stillness becomes a gift we offer the world."

Inhaled in the Mountain Air

"Sometimes, truth is not spoken—it's simply breathed in with the morning mist."

It occurs at all times

"Recognise that death is not an arbitrary event that takes place as we die at a certain stage. It occurs at all times in our lives!"

Kindred in Becoming

"We were strangers when we came. We left as witnesses of each other's unfolding."

Last breath

"Man breathes when the Supreme's prana (life breath) passes through his bodily mould, but he is no longer a living thing when that prana withdraws itself."

Last day

"It alludes to the day when one's soul departs from the transient body (Deha), and he who sent you on this plane is now welcoming you back with relief, comfort, and celebration."

Let the World Wait

"Before we return to our routines, let us sit a little longer in who we've become."

Life

"Slumber and death; Waking and birth; have proximity to live."

Life goes on

"Life goes on, and others replace the dead. Death changes nothing."

Life in fullness

"Death is the doorway to a 'Life in fullness,' and it marks the beginning of a new and better life. It merely paves the way for a higher form of life."

Light of Life

"When you long for the supreme as much as you long for your last breath in your dire situation, we will see the light at the end."

Live your life

"Don't waste your time living the life of someone else."

Living the Attraction

"When your inner world and outer actions harmonise, you radiate a magnetic light—one that not only draws abundance but leaves a legacy of inspiration for generations to come."

Long Journey

"Death is not a denial of life, but a process of life; our evolution is not complete, but continues."

Nothing dies

"Nothing ever truly dies; it simply ceases to exist in one form before resuming another."

Origin of life

"Life denotes the beginning of dying, and death denotes the origin of life."

Presence Holds the Power

"You don't need more time—you need more presence. Every sacred life begins with a Ritual Rewrites Reality: "Change doesn't begin in the world. It begins in the way you begin your morning."
Frequency Forms the Field: "Reality doesn't rise to meet your effort. It bends to the vibration you hold in your heart."

Realisation

"Like all rivers, eventually leads to the sea, life leads towards the realised one."

Rises to live

"Life is death, and death is life; whoever is born dies, and whoever dies rises to live."

Sacred Agreements

"Not every bond needs a name; some are sealed in the silence of mutual knowing."

Sacred Surrender

"Healing is not always loud or heroic. Sometimes, it is a quiet surrender to light after a long darkness."

Sacred is the Shattered

"What breaks you also blesses you, if held in the arms of grace."

Salvation

"He must move beyond that grief and suffering to seek the path of salvation."

Soul

"Though the physical appearance changes, the soul remains constant. In this way, everything changes around us, but nothing ever changes. The essence was always the same."

Soul migrates

"Death is a simple process in which a soul migrates from one Deha (body) to another."

Soul migration

"Death is a simple process in which a soul migrates from one Deha (physical being) to another based on predestined Karmic baggage."

Still Breathing, Still Becoming

"You survived not to return to the old, but to become something sacred and new."

Stillness Is Strategy

"You don't always need a plan. Sometimes you need silence—because wisdom often enters through the door that hustle overlooks."

The Echo of Intention

"The Law of Attraction is the whisper of the cosmos; the Power of Manifestation is the echo you choose to return."

The Grace of Being Witnessed

"Sometimes, the deepest healing comes not from being understood, but simply from being seen in your truth."

The Journal of Becoming

"When words rise from pain rather than escape it, they do not bleed—they bloom."

The Light That Waited

"The light within you never truly fades—it simply waits in silence until you are ready to open your eyes again."

The Open Portal

"When your intention is clear and your heart is open, miracles become the norm."

The Quiet Pilgrimage

"Healing does not arrive with noise or spectacle—it walks in barefoot, at its own pace, asking only for your presence."

The Soul Hears Repetition

"Transformation does not come from inspiration alone. It comes from the echoes of what you choose to repeat every single day."

The Space Between Words

"In the pauses of our speech, we heard the voice of something greater."

The Universe Mirrors Your Inner World

"The universe doesn't follow your words—it follows your being. And your being is sculpted by the emotions you carry."

The Weight of a Flame

"A single candle, held in sincerity, can illuminate the spaces we feared were lost forever."

The secret of death

"Our quality of life will be different if we discover the secret of death! Our perspectives of life, our comprehension of death, and our attitude towards it will change."

The shell of bondage

"Prana can leave this body at any time, just as a bird discards its shell of bondage's shell."

Thoughts

"The clouds in the sky are analogous to our thoughts! Both are constantly changing - clouds don't think; they just drift away."

Transform

"If you have planted seeds of good thoughts in the young minds, their future will progressively transform the world!"

True Departures Begin Inside

"The real journey doesn't begin when we leave the retreat—but when we carry it within."

Ultimate truth

"A true Master dispels the darkness of ignorance and leads the individual to the ultimate truth."

Unity of life

"The state of being conscious of the undivided 'unity of life,' seeing, hearing, and knowing nothing else, is known as the infinite. Beyond death, the infinite exists."

Unwritten Prayers

"Sometimes, our most sincere prayers are not spoken aloud but felt in the heartbeats of quiet moments."

What the Fire Knows

"A fire remembers every story whispered to it in vulnerability. So does the soul."

When Light Returns

"It is not always grand revelations that change us. Sometimes, it is the quiet knowing that the light will return—and so will we."

When Listening Heals

"Listening is not a passive act—it is the soul leaning close, holding another's pain without fixing it."

When the Soul Takes Form

"To wish is to dream with your eyes closed; to manifest is to walk your dream with your soul awake."

Wholeness Within Fragments

"You may never return to who you were, but in honouring your brokenness, you become someone more whole."

Your path

"The path we take after death is determined by what we did while we were living and treading on."

Divinity

Overcoming Obstacles

"Obstacles are not roadblocks, but invitations to grow. They put us to the test, showing us that the greatest victories often come from the most difficult conflicts."

- Shree Shambav

Divinity

A Lantern Within

"You are not waiting for the world to light you—you are remembering that you already burn."

Acceptance

"Accept situations without hesitation and allow things to flow naturally in whatever direction they want."

Actual language

"God's language is empathy, compassion, kindness, and silence."

Atma to Paramatma

"Like all rivers, they will eventually lead to the sea."

Atman

"I am not this skin, this flesh, this bone, this hair, or this other physical component; rather, I am the soul that resides there."

Complete surrender

"Complete surrender and devotion culminate in supreme awareness."

Confinement

"Why do you continue to live in confinement when the door is so wide open?"

Cosmos

"You are a microcosm within this vast macrocosm."

Descended

"We all have descended to the faraway land known as the earth realm, bearing the almighty's blessing and potential."

Devotion in Motion

"Let each step be a dance, not a duty; a hymn, not a hustle."

Dissolve into one

"There are a thousand different ways to get home. Just dance and celebrate until you dissolve into one."

Divine

"When the river meets the ocean, it recognises that it was the ocean from the beginning till the end. Likewise, when a self-surrender to the higher self occurs, the self becomes the 'Divine.'"

Embers of the Soul

"There is an ember in you that doesn't flicker with fear—it only waits for your still gaze to awaken it."

Enlightenment

"The path to enlightenment is of selfless devotion. For those who have achieved the pinnacle, the path is bliss, quietude, transparency, and peace."

Every Atman

"Through everything and every Atma in this universe, you can see Param-Atma."

Everything has a reason

"He provides you with what you require, declines your request for something better, tells you to wait, and then provides you with the best."

Faith is a Gentle Wait

"Surrender is not defeat—it is a sacred patience that trusts the timing of the unseen."

From Devotion to Being

"You no longer need to do devotion when you have become it."

Healing Without Words

"In the silence between words, the heart learns to breathe again."

Hollowed to Hold Light

"Sometimes life must hollow us completely—so we can hold the light we've been seeking outside ourselves."

Invisible Miracles

"The moments you think don't matter often become someone else's turning point."

Micro-Movements, Cosmic Ripples

"The universe listens not to size, but to sincerity—start small, start sacred."

More Than Doing

"Your deepest breakthroughs won't come when you try harder, but when you listen deeper."

Movement as Prayer

"When action rises from the soul, even the smallest step becomes sacred."

Not All Healing is Loud

"Some healing arrives like thunder, but most comes like morning dew—silent, soft, consistent."

Path of salvation

"To pursue the path of salvation, he has to move beyond the mundane life and worries."

Perceive

"How we perceive supreme reflects how we perceive ourselves."

Presence is Power

"Your presence is not passive. It is the soil where clarity and transformation silently take root."

Pure bliss

"There is no world in profound slumber because we are resting in the Supreme Soul. It proves the presence of the Supreme Soul, the primary nature of which is pure bliss."

Realisation

"I realise I am still raw, and I have to be cooked to know the Real."

Realm

"When I am silent, I enter a realm where everything is harmonious, tranquil, colourful, and beautiful."

Reason

"God has a reason for the misery undergone, a reason for the toil, and a reward for your devotion. Believe that the Almighty brings the right people into your life at the right time and for the right reasons."

Reason for everything

"Under His creation, there would be a reason for everything."

Sacred Smallness

"The size of the act doesn't define its divinity—its sincerity does."

Sacred Surrender

"Surrender is not defeat; it is the doorway to your truest strength."

Sacred Surrender

"Surrender is not giving up; it is laying down your burdens to walk freely with the divine."

Sacrifice and Soul

"To gain what is eternal, the temporary must sometimes be sacrificed."

Salvation

"Salvation is the essence and birthright of the soul."

Soul

"The soul is none other than God, the Brahman."

Superior soul

"When you realise you are nothing more than a part of a superior soul, stop discriminating and disliking one another, you lose your greed and desire, and you lose all worth in this materialistic world."

The Art of Letting Be

"Letting go is not losing—it's the sacred art of returning to what you never truly left."

The Door to Infinity

"You don't find the infinite in lifetimes—only in this single breath."

The Drop That Echoes

"What matters is not how much you carry, but the grace with which you offer it."

The Echo of Belief

"What you deeply believe becomes the echo the universe returns to you."

The Fire Beneath Still Ash

"Even in your quietest seasons, the ember of your soul still burns, waiting for breath to rise again."

The Fire That Waits

"Purpose is not chased—it reveals itself in the ashes of what no longer serves."

The Forgotten Church

"Every tree is a hymn, every river a sermon—nature never stopped speaking to us."

The Healer Within

"When you choose to stay, to love, to listen—you become a healer, even if you never meant to be one."

The Humble Light

"It's often the cracked, forgotten, unnoticed things that teach us how to shine without permission."

The Mirror of the Divine

"When we love without needing to fix, we reflect the face of God."

The Myth of Monumental

"Not every sacred act is loud. Some are as soft as breath—and just as vital."

The Path of Quiet Faith

"Walk the path where results don't dictate devotion. That's where miracles begin."

The Power of Presence

"You don't have to heal the world. Sometimes, just sitting beside someone in silence is enough to remind them they're not alone."

The Pulse of Heaven

"To touch another's sorrow without turning away is to speak the language of stars."

The Quiet Courage

"To speak your truth without wounding—this is the heart's highest art."

The Quiet Flame

"Gratitude is not born in comfort but in the ashes of what we almost lost."

The Ritual of Belonging

"You don't need to be understood by all, only held by a few who see you truly."

The Sacred Step

"A single action taken in joy carries more power than a thousand driven by pressure."

The Silent Teacher

"Sometimes silence teaches what scriptures never can."

The Song Beneath Silence

"True freedom is not the absence of walls, but the presence of wings within."

The Soul Knows the Shortcut

"Logic plans the long road. But the soul, in one aligned moment, takes you straight to the door."

The Soul's First Language

"Joy is not indulgent—it's the native language of your soul calling you home."

The Unowned Path

"True freedom is when even the path doesn't own you."

The Unseen Strength

"Stillness is not the absence of action—it is the presence of total clarity."

The Voice Between Beats

"In stillness, even time kneels and listens."

The Whisper of Awakening

"Pain is not punishment—it's the echo of your soul asking you to remember."

The Wing in Darkness

"Faith isn't knowing—it's flying blind into the storm and trusting the wind."

The beauty of prayer

"It only takes a sincere call as a prayer to change everything; God listens to your heart, even if you cannot put your prayer into words."

The goal of life

"The sun's reflection merges with the sun itself as the water in the pond absorbs it. Similarly, when thoughts are decimated through rumination, the individual Atma merges with the supreme soul. This is the goal of life, and one can experience it right now, while still alive."

The prayer

"When you pray to the Almighty, He responds immediately and gives you what you desire. He delays and gives you better than what you want. He prolongs, but he gives you the best you ever expected."

Unseen Ripening

"There is a grace unfolding in your silence that no effort can hurry and no fear can delay."

When Nothing is Something

"When you don't know what to say, your presence can become the most eloquent prayer."

Where Joy Points, Follow

"The emotion behind your movement defines its momentum. Let lightness lead."

Karma

Reflections on Identity and Purpose

"In the mirror of introspection, we find the reflection of our true self, and in the journey to understand it, we uncover the purpose that gives our life meaning."

- Shree Shambav

Actions

"What you give to others always comes back to you."

Attachment

"As one thinks about the objects of the senses, one becomes attached to them. Attachment comes before desire, and desire comes before anger."

Cause and effect

"Every action, thought and feeling is motivated by an intention having the cause and effect embedded within."

Compassion

"If you sow kindness, you reap friendship, and if you sow compassion, you reap love."

Destiny

"We are in charge of our destiny and control our future by how we think and act."

Dharma

"The quintessence of Dharma is peacefulness, truth, non-coveting, an immaculate mind and body, and the control of all faculties."

Each verdict

"Each verdict depicts how an individual is mainly responsible for his actions."

Effort

"What we want comes from participation; life does not happen by itself; we must make it happen."

Fruits of Karma

"Every moment of our lives, we are not only living the fruits of our previous actions, but also creating those for tomorrow."

Greatest successes

"Your greatest successes in life will often come from assisting others in their endeavours."

Hope

"If the fruit is your hope, you're Good Karma. If you do not expect it, then it is your bad Karma."

How do you react?

"An individual's Karma is determined by how they treat you, but your karma is determined by how you react."

Humility

"Before we can change our current circumstances, we must accept them and take life as it comes."

Intertwined

"Everyone is intertwined with the past, present, and future."

Karma

"Everyone is inextricably linked to the past, present, and future."

Light

"Eternal Light is something that has always existed. The amount of light you receive will depend on your actions."

Master your actions

"By liberating ourselves from ego and illusion, we can become masters of our actions."

Our actions

"All of our lives are the consequence of our efforts and actions."

Our behaviour

"The fruits of past Karma will manifest itself in every moment and behaviour of our everyday lives."

Past Karma

"The fruits of past Karma will show up in every moment and behaviour in our daily life."

Prarabdha

"No one can share your Prarabdha or reduce your Karma."

Reap

"If you plant love and kindness, you will reap what you sow."

Reward

"The best reward comes from our collective effort and energy."

Samskara

"Samskara is an addiction pattern. As long as the Samskara is alive, it's bound to recur, and the person suffers because of that."

Seed

"Because like begets like, a paddy seed cannot create wheat. Accordingly, every living being develops in the present pattern of life as determined by the seed's inherent nature."

Seed of Destiny

"Actions are the seed of destiny."

The cycle of Karma

"We end up caught in the cycle of Karma when our actions are motivated by desire and greed."

Thoughts and actions

"Our behaviour should correspond to our thoughts and actions."

Unreturned

"The Law of Karma states that neither a drop of kindness nor a speck of evil will go unreturned."

Your actions

"Your Karma is your action and making."

Learning is Treasure

Nurturing Connections

"In the garden of life, connections are blooming flowers, and nurturing them is the tender touch that allows beauty to flourish."

- *Shree Shambav*

Learning is Treasure

A lie

"Lies may last a few hours, but the truth will last forever."

A wise person

"A wise person is the one who can forgive others."

Accept with grace

"Life is a series of natural and unanticipated changes. Don't fight them; instead, accept them with grace."

Anchor of Identity

"When you affirm from who you are, not who you wish you were, your words become anchors, not illusions."

Appreciate the Earth

"If you want your children to be loving and compassionate, allow them to appreciate the earth and care for the living beings around them."

Better view

"When the mountain is shrouded in clouds, dressed in snow, and painted in golden yellow, the journey appears difficult, tedious, and rough. However, as we reach the top and look down, we take a deep breath of fresh air. The perspective changes, and we soon understand there are a million other ways to get there. And we found the best view at the summit of the most challenging ascent."

Blooming

"Every flower represents a soul blooming with beauty and innocence."

Burden

"Expectation leads to dependency, and the dependency leads to burden or bondage."

Choice

"It is your choice whether you laugh or cry; it is your life."

Coexistence

"When considering coexistence, two words spring to mind: coexistence and harmony. Nature is full of life and energy, and everything is in balance there. All sentient beings, except for humans, coexist in harmony. We, Humans, wreak havoc on the habitat, which will lead to disaster, eventually."

Delusion

"This place is a fantasy or delusion. The only person who thinks it is true is asleep. Death then appears like the dawn, and you awaken laughing at what you had mistaken for grief."

Desire

"The most contented man is one who has control over his desires."

Different

"There are many trees and beings around, and no two leaves or life forms are alike; similarly, no journey on the same path would be alike."

Do not grieve!

"Do not grieve! Everything you lose eventually comes back to you in some other way."

Emotion

The Unseen Sculptor: "Your emotions carve the shape of tomorrow—each feeling is a chisel, each vibration a hand guiding your fate."

Essence

"The wise person embraces the essence of various scriptures and only sees well in them, similar to how a butterfly flutters over many flowers to taste its essence."

Experience

"A wealth of experience fortifies the ability to arrive at sound decisions."

Faith

"Your trials keep you strong! Human, your sorrows will keep you alive! Failure teaches you humility! You will continue to shine because of your success! But faith is the only thing that keeps you going."

Fly

"I'm not scared of failing. I simply do not know how to fly."

Good deed

"A tree can be remembered by its fruits and blooms, whereas a man can be identified only by his actions. A good deed is never forgotten, but a wicked act will always come back to haunt."

In-between

"We came from the earth; we shall return to the dirt - bloom, fade, and wilt in between."

Inferior

"Without your permission, they cannot judge you inferior."

Learn

"Learn how to listen and understand better those who speak negatively about you."

Letting the Heart Be Held

"Some wounds do not need to be healed—they only ask to be held without shame."

Living Language

"A real affirmation is not spoken—it is lived. It breathes in your choices, not just your voice."

Mind is everything

"The mind is everything in this world. It is the source of all pain and suffering. If the mind can be healed, all illnesses in this world will be cured."

Misery

"We are solely to blame for our misery."

Momentum in the Small Steps

"Every small victory is a stone laid on the path to your greatest dreams."

A more beautiful place

"Without water, there is no life. We define conservation as maintaining a state of equilibrium between living things and the natural world. Let us live a cleaner life by making the world more beautiful."

Most beautiful

"A breeze carries the fragrance of the flower, and flowers giveth to the world fragrance and beauty, even though they fade, wilt, and wither in a day."

Nature's law

"Plant the seeds of love, kindness, empathy, and compassion, and they will return to you in abundance, according to nature's law."

Our mind

"Our minds are constantly filled with self-doubts and internal conflicts that accuse us of being helpless, miserable, stupid, and deceived."

Pain is a Portal

"Pain, when honoured instead of feared, becomes the very portal to awakening."

Realise

"Give everything you've got; in the end, you'll realise you owned nothing at all."

Slay your enemy

"You should slay your enemy called lust through the knowledge of self. Once you realise this truth, you will find happiness."

Solace

"If you're scared, lonely, unhappy, or sad, go for a walk through the woods and fields, along the coast and rivers, or through the mountains and sea. Nature will provide solace in any situation."

Stillness is a Teacher

"There are lessons only stillness can teach—when you stop trying to fix the pain and simply feel it."

Stories That Heal Us All

"True stories do not belong to one heart—they live in the collective soul, healing all who are willing to listen."

Thank them

"If you cannot appreciate others, at the very least, thank them."

The Compass Within

"When your intent is clear, the path appears—not because the world changes, but because you finally know where to look."

The Fragrance of Feeling

"If your affirmation carries no feeling, it is a script. If it carries soul, it becomes sacred."

The Garden Within

"Your mind is a garden; your thoughts are the seeds. You can grow flowers or you can grow weeds—but you must live with what blooms."

The Lens of Desire

"Unclear intent is like looking through fogged glass—clean the lens, and even the distant horizon begins to shine."

The Mirror of the Mind

"Reality is not a separate entity—it is your reflection in motion, sculpted by what you dare to believe is true."

The Power of Persistent Flow

"Dedication is not rigid resistance—it is the gentle, unwavering current that carries you forward."

The Silence That Speaks

"Some silences are not empty—they are full of all the words the soul cannot yet say."

The Whisper of Worth

"Even a whisper spoken in truth carries more power than the loudest shout rooted in fear."

Thoughts

"Green is more valuable and beautiful, and a positive person notices it everywhere. You will continue to grow as long as your thoughts are green."

Thoughts That Tremble the Air

"Every thought is a silent wave cast into the ocean of reality—rippling outward to meet you again as life."

Transformation Wears Silence

"Real transformation doesn't always roar. Sometimes it walks in barefoot, covered in silence."

Trust

"Faith isn't blind belief; it's unwavering trust."

Ultimate truth

"All you have is yourself, and that is the ultimate truth."

Vision That Breathes

"A dream defined becomes a map; a goal envisioned with soul becomes a living force that breathes you forward."

Wants

"We are busy chasing, not knowing what exactly we want?"

Wealth

"Wealth comes like a turtle and leaves like the wind."

Wisdom of nature

"Seek the wisdom of nature through the eyes of a child."

Your Voice, Your Vow

"Let your affirmation be your voice's vow to your future self—spoken not to impress, but to express alignment."

Your actions

"Hastiness leads to regret, but patience and empathy lead to peace and happiness."

Life Insights

Empowering the Mind and Spirit

"Empowering the mind and spirit is the journey to free ourselves from the shackles of limitation, allowing us to soar on the wings of our potential."

- Shree Shambav

Life Insights

A beggar

"A beggar will always be a beggar, even if you give him the entire world."

A true beggar

"A true beggar is unaware of his real wealth hidden deep within."

A woman

"Nothing is impossible in this world for a woman because she is born with the determination to make it happen."

Accept

"It is not possible to plan your future based on your past, and you cannot live your present life thinking about the future. Just accept as life takes you."

Acceptance

"Whatever life throws at you, what you make of it is entirely left to you."

Be unique

"You must sacrifice if you want to be unique."

Beautiful things

"The most beautiful things are unseen but can be felt."

Belief Shapes the Invisible

"What you truly believe in your heart and subconscious mind creates the blueprint for your reality."

Beyond What Eyes Can See

"The most vital parts of your journey happen in the invisible. Honour what the world overlooks."

Clarity Through Stillness

"Stillness is not the absence of movement; it is the beginning of understanding."

Confidence is the Bridge

"Self-belief is the bridge between desire and manifestation—it carries your dreams from thought into form."

Desire with Surrender

"Let your desires breathe. Don't cage them with control—trust that their wings know the sky."

Detach to Receive

"Hold the vision gently, like a bird in your palm. Clutch too tight, and it loses its wings."

Determination

"A man moves a mountain carrying small stones."

Energy Doesn't Lie

"Your thoughts speak. Your emotions shout. But your energy—your energy tells the whole truth."

Eternal time

"Life is an eternal time in motion."

Faith

"If you lose faith in yourself, you lose faith in success. As achievers, your fall is obvious."

Faith Beyond Logic

"Logic builds roads. Faith builds wings."

Fear

"Fear of failing is the root of all jealousy."

Fear

"Letting go of fear is the key to change."

First step

"You'll figure it out. All you have to do now is take the first step."

Freedom

"Freedom will always be accompanied by accountability."

From Scarcity to Sacredness

"Gratitude turns what you have into a blessing and what you lack into peace."

Good deeds

"Your life's lesson should be written not in words, but in good deeds."

Growth

"As learning has no end, even inner growth and progress have no end."

Guard

"Our mouth should be guarded by three criteria: truthfulness, empathy and necessity."

Invisible Architecture

"Every moment of inner faith is laying invisible bricks beneath the life you're building."

Invisible Work

"What appears stagnant on the surface may be a soul preparing its roots for sacred growth beneath."

Life is beautiful

"I walked through the woods and fields, the coastline and rivers, the mountains and sea, and the earth and sky. I realised that life is full of beauty after seeing the flying bees, the fragrance of flowers, the smell of rain, the soft touch of the wind, the roaring waves, and the flashing stars."

Listen

"Listen to what is said rather than who is speaking."

Love

"Let us spread love in honour of the word 'love' and its 'strength.'"

Magnet of the Heart

"What you feel in your core becomes the frequency you emit—and what you emit is what you attract."

Make it a reality

"If you have a dream, don't let it go unfulfilled. Gather the courage to believe in your ability to succeed and make the necessary plans to make it a reality."

Mind and love

"Mind and love are not compositions of the same entity."

My lovely parents

"When my mother gave me wings to fly, my father broadened the horizons for me to fly."

Need

"The person with the least needs is the richest; not the one with the most possessions."

Openness

"You should openly speak about sins and wrongdoings committed."

Perpetuity

"What we do for ourselves ultimately perishes, whereas what we do for others exists in perpetuity."

Pride

"My pride fell with my fortunes."

Resilience is Remembering

"Resilience is not how loudly you bounce back—it's how quietly you remember your worth."

Rest Is Not Retreat

"Pausing does not mean quitting. Even the sun rests before it rises again."

Rest as a Sacred Action

"When you rest with trust, it is not idleness—it is a deep conversation with the future."

Rewrite Your Inner Story

"Changing your story is not about pretending—it's about awakening to the truth that you are already powerful beyond measure."

Rewriting the Script

"Every time you choose a higher thought, you rewrite the story of who you are becoming—one sentence closer to joy."

Sagacity

"Turn your tribulations into lessons and your lessons into sagacity."

Simple equation

"Life is a simple equation: if you think you can't do anything, you won't be able to. You can do it if you believe you can."

Skill

"You can achieve the pinnacle with minimal skill if you are dedicated to what you are doing."

Smile

"Show life that you have a million ways to smile when it gives you a thousand reasons to cry."

Soul Before Strategy

"No strategy will succeed when the soul is missing. Alignment is not a plan—it is a presence."

Still Waters, Strong Currents

"When your inner sea is calm, even the faintest vision can sail far—guided by the wind of aligned emotion."

Success

"If you want to lift yourself, uplift others."

The Circle of Community

"The people around you are not background—they are mirrors, magnifiers, and messengers."

The Compass of Joy

"The truest path may not be the hardest—but the one where joy quietly returns, even when things are unclear."

The Currency of Attention

"Where your attention flows, your reality follows. Spend it like sacred currency."

The Echo and the Origin

"An affirmation without ownership is merely an echo—it mimics strength but lacks the soul of its origin."

The Echo of Emotion

"The universe does not respond to your words—it responds to the emotional tone beneath them."

The Fire Beneath Stillness

"The universe does not move on noise—it listens for the soul that burns quietly, with unwavering intent."

The Frequency of Trust

"What you expect from life often bends to what you deeply believe, not what you outwardly wish."

The Gardener of Thought

"Your mind listens to the words you plant. Speak with kindness—grow with care—and your life will bloom accordingly."

The Gentle Revolution

"Change does not always roar. Sometimes, it whispers into your habits and rewrites your entire destiny."

The Inner Soil

"You can only grow what you have made room for—remove the weeds of doubt before you sow your dreams."

The Light Behind the Clouds

"Positive thinking is not denial—it is the sun you keep burning behind your storm, waiting to break through."

The Mirror Beyond Fog

"Awareness doesn't change the world—it changes the eyes that behold it."

The Mirror of Delay

"Every delay reflects a deeper readiness the universe is inviting you to uncover."

The Mirror of Delay

"What delays you often reflects what you still need to learn, not what life is denying you."

The Quiet Alchemy

"Gratitude doesn't change the world outside—it transforms how the world touches your heart."

The Truth Beyond Name

"Beneath every name, face, and form—there is only one silence."

The Unfinished Poem

"Life is not a race to complete—it's a poem we're still learning how to read."

The Unseen Shift

"Sometimes your breakthrough begins with a whisper, not a roar."

The flow of life

"Don't resist or grieve the flow of river life."

The river of life

"Never try to resist or hurry the river of life. Simply go with the flow to discover the true meaning of life."

To control

"We cannot control everything that happens around us, but we can control what happens within us."

Trust Is a Sacred Bridge

"Between intention and outcome lies trust—the bridge where miracles quietly walk."

Undisciplined mind

"An undisciplined mind is the most extraordinary of all foes."

Value

"Once you carry your pitcher of water, you will learn the value of every drop."

Life Values and Beliefs

Embracing Self-Acceptance

"Self-acceptance is the gentle rain that nourishes the roots of our worth and enables us to bloom with the beauty of our truth."

- *Shree Shambav*

A change

"By changing ourselves, we change our lives."

A moment

"Let us live for the moment."

Beneath the Repetition

"Repetition alone cannot make something true—it is the feeling beneath it that makes it real."

Bitterness

"Bitterness fruit is an acid that eats away at its container."

Boundless

"He who picks the endless has effectively been picked by the boundless."

Cycle

"Life is eternal as time progresses from eternity to eternity, in one form after another, appearing, disappearing, and reappearing like waves on the sea."

Deserve

"You deserve everything excellent this world has to give and nothing less."

Desire

"Many things will seem few if you desire many things."

Devoid

"A life devoid of affection is like a tree devoid of its bloom or fruit."

Do not cling

"We cannot be in the present if we are still clinging to our past."

Echoes

"They returned our actions and words to us like echoes in a mountain."

Effort

"Our lives are entirely the result of our efforts."

Empathy and compassion

"Empathy is the language of the blind who can see, and compassion is the music of the deaf who can hear."

Fear Transformed Into Flow

"When you stop fighting change, you allow life's river to carry you to new and wondrous shores."

Focus

"We can't simultaneously think of two things."

Fortitude

"Until you have the fortitude to lose sight of the coast, you cannot swim for new vistas."

Freedom

"True freedom comes from not getting confined or attached to any object, activity, or situation."

Greed

"For greed, all abundance is insufficient."

Growth Lives Outside Comfort

"True transformation begins when you choose growth over the safety of familiarity."

Happiness

"Nobody can take your happiness away once you learn how to create it."

History continues

"History continues until we learn from it and change our course."

Hope

"Yesterday was not ours, but tomorrow is."

Human nature

"We all think our minds are very logical but perceive them to be very illogical as well."

Innocence

"I'm delighted I could reclaim part of my childhood innocence and beauty."

Just sing

"If you want to sing, you sing without considering who is listening or what they might think."

Life is a journey

"Life is a journey . . . yearning for love."

Life value

"When a hungry man eats, and a tired man sleeps, we realise true life values."

Lifestyle

"The choice is yours..., choose the way you want to live!"

Make it happen

"What we want comes from our participation in activities and indulging in it; life does not happen by itself; we must make it happen."

The mind is the source

"The mind is the source of all suffering; it starts all activity, whether a charity, performing one's duties, or performing nothing at all."

Move When the Heart Says Yes

"The right time to act is when your heart expands, not contracts. Momentum begins with truth, not urgency."

Music

"Life is celestial music, an unwritten poem, and an unfathomable love story."

Participation

"What we seek in life results from our participation. Life does not happen by itself; we must make it so."

Past and future

"Each saint has a past; each sinner has a future."

Perseverance

"The most valuable reward entailed perseverance."

Procrastination Is the Absence of Inner Alignment

"You're not lazy—you're just not aligned. When your why is soul-deep, your how reveals itself."

Ripples

"Just as ripples spread when a single pebble is dropped onto the tranquil water."

Rooted Belief

"Words grow only when rooted in belief. Without roots, affirmations wilt in the silence of disbelief."

Seed of the Soul

"True affirmations are seeds planted in the soil of self-awareness and watered with patience and practice."

Silent Ingredients

"Every silent belief you rehearse in the dark becomes the recipe for the Truth Doesn't Perform: "An affirmation isn't a performance for the universe; it's a vow whispered from the self to the self."

Teamwork

"The best reward comes from our collective effort and energy."

The Gift Hidden in Uncertainty

"Within every unknown lies a seed of possibility waiting to bloom."

The Mirror Ritual

"Before you affirm who you are, take time to see yourself—really see yourself."

The Paper Flower

"A borrowed affirmation is like a paper flower—pleasing to the eye but absent of fragrance or life."

The Whisper Over the Roar

"Inspired action doesn't shout—it whispers through the soul. Ego demands speed, but intuition invites grace."

The beauty of Life

"Live the moment; know the beauty of this life."

True bliss

"We can make a difference in the world by having a sympathetic perspective, listening with empathy, speaking with compassion, loving with our hearts, and performing acts of kindness. Develop it to realise the true bliss of life."

Wheel of life

"Everything supervenes a cycle."

Look Deep into Nature!

Finding Joy in the Present

"In the garden of now, joy is the vibrant bloom we pluck, its fragrance a reminder that life's beauty is woven into each passing moment."

- *Shree Shambav*

A glimmer of hope

"Throw yourself into nature's arms when you're completely lost in the dark; it will reveal a new glimmer of hope."

A movement

"Love for Mother Nature has sparked a movement."

A tree

"Trees inspire, roots provide drive, and leaves provide perpetual change."

Beware

"Nothing can ever fix Mother Nature, not even all power and money in this world."

Change

"It is critical that change occurs before it is too late."

Colourful

"Take a deep dive into nature. You will see everything around you colourful."

Deeper

"Your understanding of life will deepen as you spend more time in nature."

Delicate

"Man is as tough as a rock but delicate as a flower."

Disappear into

"Every time I admire nature, I wish I could just disappear into it."

Don't Rush the Flame

"A rushed fire burns out. A patient one warms the soul."

Glow Without Proof

"You don't need visible results to trust your inner fire. Some lights are felt before they're seen."

Happiness

"The blowing wind, the running river, the craggy mountains, the thick forest, and the clear sky all contribute to my happiness."

Held by the Earth

"There is a grace in sitting on the ground of your grief, knowing the earth will not let you fall further."

Inner Weather

"You don't carry your past—you carry your interpretation of it. And that can change with one clear breath."

It teaches

"Nature teaches us to be compassionate, kind, and non-discriminatory."

It transforms

"Nature is a vast reservoir of life where energy is always conserved and cannot be created or destroyed."

Just listen

"Listen to the ripple and feel what it smells like and what it tells you."

Law of nature

"If a child puts his hand in the fire out of ignorance, the fire will still burn the child, regardless of his innocence."

Light

"We appreciate the light after stumbling around in the dark."

Magnificent

"Clouds above clouds, what a spectacular sight against the deep blue sky!"

Miracles

"If you look at nature closely, you will notice miracles all around you."

Mother Nature

"Waterfalls are a magnificent creation of Mother Nature."

Moving mist

"As I stood there watching the mist softly rise, I wondered what vista could be more beautiful than this. The dense mist obscured visibility at times. The wind howled and roared as it swept through."

My understanding

"The brisk wind, flowing river, rocky mountains, dense forest, and blue sky all contribute to my deep understanding of life."

Once in a lifetime

"Every individual has the power to make a positive impact on the environment; planting a tree is a simple yet meaningful way to do so."

One's search

"Nature's serene beauty and tranquillity aid in one's search."

Perfect traveller

"A perfect traveller who, as it flows, overcomes all obstacles. It cuts through the rock, flows through the meadows, crosses the dense forest, clears all dirt in its path, and sets off on its wonderful adventure."

Plant

"Once in a lifetime, everyone should plant a tree at least once."

Precious

"Every glittering stone, like every shining metal, is not precious."

Presence of beauty

"When you are in the beauty's presence of nature, nothing but happiness can overtake you."

Promise

"Each morning, the sun promises a new beginning, a chance to chase our dreams and leave the darkness behind."

Recognise

"Newborns are to our planet what stars are to the sky. They deserve to be recognised!"

Reflection

"Oh! My hand carefully laid you on this earth, soulful-looking beauties. You are charmed by the magnificence with which you are enthralled. Is it my soulful reflection or your beauty that draws me to you?"

Regrettable

"Regrettably, we believe we own the earth, the trees, the mountains, flowing rivers, and many other things, but we are all owned by nature."

Roots Before Bloom

"Let your belief grow deeper than your fear—roots before blossoms, always."

Source of happiness

"Simply go outside and have fun. The most abundant source of happiness is nature."

Still Waters Speak

"Clarity is not created through force. It is revealed when the mind becomes quiet enough to hear the truth."

Sunrise

"We have seen countless sunrises, but their beauty never ceases to amaze us."

The Garden Beneath Thought

"Lasting change begins where no one sees—beneath the thought, behind the habit, below the noise."

The Garden of Repetition

"Your habits water your beliefs. Tend them with presence, and your mind becomes a sanctuary."

The Gift in the Ashes

"What once seemed like ruin may one day be revealed as the exact fire needed to remake you."

The Soil Listens

"The subconscious does not argue—it accepts. And what you plant in silence, it grows in time."

The Trust Between Beats

"The universe speaks not only in signs, but in the spaces between them. Learn to trust the in-between."

The Whisper That Waited

"What you call a delay may just be your soul waiting for your full presence to arrive."

The rule of law

"In the past, present, and future, the rule of law is unbiased and routine."

True beauty

"We would not understand true beauty if we had not experienced the grotesqueness of life."

Truth

"Whatever we carry in our dreams will vanish as soon as we realise the truth."

Truth Rises in Still Water

"In the agitated mind, nothing reflects clearly. Truth rises only when the water is still."

Unbiased

"Nature makes no distinction between creating and destroying life."

When the River Turns

"The mind resists change the way a river resists redirection. But one stone at a time, the current shifts."

When the Wind Teaches

"Even the wind that puts out your flame teaches you which direction your light belongs to."

Whispers That Rewire

"Affirmations are not to convince the world, but to remind the self what it once forgot."

Witness

"The stars may twinkle in the sky, but they bear witness to the grief of a heartbroken man."

Wounds That Spoke First

"Most of your limiting beliefs were not born from truth—but from pain that spoke before love could."

Your Inner Sky

"Even on the darkest nights, stars exist. Sometimes your soul just needs time to clear the clouds."

Maya or Illusion

Fuelling the Soul

"To fuel the soul is to invest in the eternal. It is the heartbeat of our passions, the melody of our dreams, and the fire that keeps our spirits alive."

- Shree Shambav

Absolute self

"Under the guise of Maya, the soul has forgotten its true, real self. It is unaware that it is Atman (Self) part of Param Atman (Absolute self)."

Acts

"Birth and death are two of Maya's juggling acts. In this illusion, genesis and cessation are doors of entry and exit on the Maya stage."

Agony

"I have found a boat to cross the expanse of all common agonies."

Attachment

"External objects are not the ones that intertwine with us. It's the inner attachment that entangles us."

Breath Between Worlds

"Every breath is a bridge between the seen and the unseen—inhale presence, exhale surrender, and find yourself walking the invisible path home."

Clarity Creates Gravity

"Vague dreams float away. But clarity creates gravity—the universe pulls what you are precise about."

Deluded

"We are deluded by Maya. We are the slaves of illusion."

Dualities

"We all live in a myriad of dualities."

Energy Chooses Direction

"What you focus on doesn't just grow—it gathers momentum, meaning, and memory."

Faith in the Unseen

"Patience is the soul's way of saying, 'I trust the roots even before the bloom.'"

Forsake

"We do not have to renounce what we have; we have to forsake what we do not have."

From Scarcity to Sacredness

"Manifestation begins not with need, but with knowing you are already enough."

Illusion

"Maya deludes us; we are the slaves of illusion."

Maya

"Everything around us is an illusion that tries to deviate from the ultimate reality."

Mightier

"Maya or illusion always overpowers the soul. Does it mean that Maya is mightier?"

Nothing is permanent

"In this world of Maya, nothing is permanent, not even our pain and suffering."

Reminds

"Seek out the flower as a reminder that your time here is limited."

Roots of Stillness

"In the noise of the world, the soul often forgets its own voice. Stillness is not emptiness—it is the soil where truth takes root."

Sacred Wounds

"Pain opens the door that comfort often hides—each wound, a sacred passage through which the soul learns to feel, forgive, and finally be free."

Self-Belief Is Infrastructure

"Your dreams do not collapse from the outside. They collapse when the inner scaffolding of self-worth isn't in place."

Self-aware

"When one becomes self-aware, all mental delusions fade away like darkness in the sky, banished by the movement of the sun."

Soulful Consumption

"Not everything that enters your mind deserves a seat at your table. Protect your inner feast with discernment."

Stare

"Maya had disappeared, but she had been staring at him in entirety after the passing."

Surrender is Strength

"Letting go is not weakness. It is trusting that your soul knows the way better than your schedule does."

The Inner Altar

"Whatever you place on the altar of your attention becomes sacred. Make sure you are worshipping what empowers you."

The Inner Climate

"The storms in your life often reflect the clouds in your mind. Change the inner sky, and the world grows calm."

The Mirror of Mortality

"Death is not the end, but the mirror in which life sees itself clearly—only when we confront the shadow, do we begin to understand the light we carry."

The Rehearsal of Reality

"Visualisation isn't dreaming. It's rehearsing the truth your soul is ready to live."

The Unseen Ingredients

"The most potent energies shaping your life are the ones you repeat silently and unconsciously."

Thought as Destiny

"Every thought you entertain is a thread in the fabric of your future. Weave it with care."

True bliss

"True bliss is never experienced through the senses (Pancha jnanendriya) but exists beyond the senses."

Unfolding the Self

"Growth is not in becoming someone else, but in remembering who you were before the world told you who to be."

Vasanas (Karmic imprint)

"Right actions do not bind, but they exhaust the Vasanas. Forbidden actions bind and add to the Vasanas, and not doing any actions bind and accumulate Vasanas."

Wheel of life

"According to the wheel of life, everything is subject to change and extinction."

Your Actions Are Invitations

"The divine won't force its way in. It enters through the open door of your deliberate, daily doing."

Your Subconscious Is Listening"

"If you wouldn't speak it to a child you love, don't whisper it to yourself."

See Beyond the Veil

Dreams and Aspirations

"Passions are the stars that guide us through life's boundless darkness, illuminating our path with the light of purpose and fulfilment."

- *Shree Shambav*

A Flame, Not a Chase

"If your dream feels like a burden, it's not aligned—it should burn like purpose, not pressure."

Alignment Over Applause

"Walk not for validation, but because the direction itself feels like home."

Begin With the Next Thought

"You don't have to control every thought. Just choose the next one with love."

Beneath the Surface

"It's not the loudest thought that shapes your life, but the quiet belief you repeat when no one is listening."

Consistency Is a Spell

"Magic isn't found in moments—it's formed in the rituals you repeat with love and belief."

Deception

"Nothing corporeal is real; only the incorporeal is devoid of deception."

Desire

"The world is under the influence of adverse forces and hostile energy-filled because of desires, impulses, and mixed wills... which are beyond control and immersed in falsehood. Sorrow is the fruit yielded by humankind."

Do not reflect

"Man prefers to reflect rather than experience reality; no mirror can reflect you; you prefer reality to mirrors."

Duality

"I've buried duality. I've witnessed the merging of the two worlds."

Emotion

"Any intensely lived emotion liberates us from those very emotions themselves."

Emotion Is the Engine

"It's not the vision alone that manifests your reality. It's the feeling behind it that makes it magnetic."

Emotion Is the Ink

"Affirmations without emotion are like inkless pens—moving but not writing."

Emotions Are Teachers

"Every emotion you suppress becomes a belief you unconsciously accept."

From Habit to Healing

"A single shift in your daily ritual can become the turning point of your destiny."

Good pounding

"Even good paddy is punished by being pounded with the pestle to yield rice. Whatever life throws at you, what you make of it is entirely up to you."

Listen

"One who is too relentless to listen to other people's views finds very few people who agree with him."

Lullabies of Becoming

"The words you whisper before sleep are seeds. They bloom in the silence between dreams."

Magnet of the Heart

"The universe responds not to your words, but to the feeling behind them."

Our nature

"It's in my nature to save him, just as it's in the scorpion's nature to sting. Why should I forsake my essence, just as he does not abandon his?"

Radiant light

"When people understand the basic fact (truth), all uncertainty will vanish like darkness before the radiant light."

Reach the light

"You can't stay in the dark and think the light doesn't reach you."

Real-world

"Do you think you're in the real world? You confess that while sleeping. You do not observe the world or your existence; the world appears as soon as you wake up. So, where is it, exactly?"

Reality

"We need to understand that neither the Sun shakes nor does it get turbid."

Reflection

"One cannot reflect oneself in tumultuous and flowing water. The more turbulent the situation, the more distorted your reflection."

Roar

"You may not bleat; instead, you can roar with pride."

Say It Until You Know It

"Speak not because you believe it yet, but because you are becoming the one who does."

Silent Mirroring

"Your inner dialogue is not private—it echoes in every step you take and every choice you make."

Small Steps, Eternal Ripples

"When a small action is rooted in truth, its echo travels far beyond what the mind can measure."

The Alchemy of Gratitude

"Gratitude doesn't fix everything. It transforms the lens through which you see everything."

The Alchemy of Presence

"When you meet the moment fully, even the mundane becomes miraculous."

The Altar of Action

"The sacred is not far. It lives in the small, intentional acts that become offerings to your highest self."

The Canvas Waits for Colour

"A desire held without expression is just a sketch. Life responds when you pick up the brush and paint with action."

The Compass Within

"Inspired action doesn't come from pressure—it rises from a quiet yes deep inside your chest."

The Compass of Emotion

"Your feelings are not flaws—they are frequencies. Tune in, and they will guide you home."

The Compass of the Soul

"What you ache for is not distance—it's the echo of who you truly are."

The Daily Pilgrimage

"To keep showing up when no one's watching—that is love in its purest prayer."

The Echo of Emotion

"Your desires don't manifest by wish alone—they rise or wither in the emotion that carries them."

The First Step Is the Shift

"Putting on your shoes with joy can change the destination of your soul."

The Frequency of Becoming

"You are not waiting for your future—you are practising it through every choice you make today."

The Frequency of Faith

"Faith isn't a belief in the unseen—it's a vibration that makes the unseen start moving toward you."

The Future Feels You

"The future does not respond to your hope. It responds to your frequency—and your frequency is shaped by what you do today."

The Gentle Rebellion

"Every time you speak kindly to yourself in a world that taught you otherwise, you rebel with grace."

The Hidden Gold

"You don't need more to feel more—just fewer distractions between you and the sky."

The Home Within

"You don't need to fit in to belong—you need only to remember you are already whole."

The Mirror Doesn't Lie

"Your self-image is the script. Life merely plays it out."

The Mirror Moves

"The world outside doesn't shift until the mirror inside is cleaned. Your perception is the prophecy."

The Present Is the Paintbrush

"Dreams are not drawn from the future. They are painted from the pigments of your daily presence."

The Quiet Revolution

"Transforming your life doesn't begin with thunder. It begins with a single breath, believed in."

The Reclamation of Light

"Healing is the slow return of your soul to its own voice."

The Sacred Signal

"Loneliness is not emptiness—it's your soul longing to sit beside itself."

The Softest Work is the Deepest

"Changing your mind doesn't look heroic from the outside. But it is inner warfare with peace as its prize."

The Sparrow's Courage

"Even a single drop carried with love is a rebellion against helplessness."

The Unseen Architect

"Your outer world is the sculpture. But your inner beliefs are the hands holding the chisel."

The Untamed Light

"Awareness isn't a concept—it's the wild flame that burns illusion to ash."

The Veil Torn Gently

"Awakening isn't becoming someone new—it's remembering you were never asleep."

Truth

"You are nearing the grave, but still running for a worry-free life and happiness."

You Are the Portal

"Destiny does not knock on your door. It walks through the portal you become when you align with your soul."

Your Voice, Reclaimed

"Reprogramming is not brainwashing. It is soul-reminding."

To Achieve in Life

Turning Challenges into Growth

"Like a phoenix rising from the ashes, our truest growth emerges from the fires of life's trials, forging us into stronger, wiser beings."

- Shree Shambav

Achieve goals

"Silence is the most effective tool for accomplishing goals."

Becoming the Prayer

"Do not pray for love while vibrating in fear. Become the emotion of what you desire—and the universe will answer through form."

Becoming the Sanctuary

"Sometimes, your soul is not the seeker—it is the sanctuary for those who've been seeking too long."

Before You Choose

"Pause not to ask what the right decision is, but to ask what feeling is guiding you to it."

Begin Without Burden

"Let today's beginning not be about outcome, but about honesty."

Beneath the Surface

"The universe doesn't strip you down to break you—it does so to show you your roots."

Between Doubt and Becoming

"Your truest affirmation may tremble when first spoken—but that tremble is the sound of becoming."

Borrowed Mantras, Forgotten Selves

"We lose ourselves not in silence, but in mantras we never took the time to believe."

Clay and Flame

"You are both the potter and the clay—shaped by fire, refined by touch."

Coexist

"Happiness and sufferings coexist on the wheel of life."

Coffee

"Nothing is more scrumptious than a cup of bitter coffee."

Content

"The greatest accomplishment is to be content."

Decide

"Now decide whether to bemoan the circumstance or celebrate the present because they have all gone for good."

Emotion Is the Author

"Every decision is not born from logic, but from the emotion that held your hand before you chose."

Emotional Frequency

"Emotions are not just reactions—they are frequencies. They call in people, patterns, and possibilities."

Faith

"Faith is the power that allows a perplexing world to emerge into the light."

Feeding Tomorrow

"Every moment you choose a thought, you are feeding tomorrow's outcome. Choose like your future depends on it—because it does."

Freedom in Detachment

"When you release the need to control the how and when, you open the door for miracles to enter."

Frequency Is Fate

"The emotions you entertain today are quietly arranging the meetings, moments, and miracles of tomorrow."

Greed

"Greed is the source of all suffering and pain."

Grief Has No Language

"When someone's heart is broken, they don't need your words—they need your willingness to stay."

Grief as Gatekeeper

"Before growth, there is grief. Before bloom, a burial."

Happy life

"We are what we think, so we live with our thoughts. To live a happy life, think positively."

In the Wake of Ashes

"What is lost outside may awaken what was always asleep within."

Innocence

"Bring back your innocence and let the child who still lives within us realise the difference between right and wrong. Connect with beauty, ignore ugliness, and be cautious about what you absorb in your body and mind. Eventually, nothing is more precious than an innocent child's heart."

Inside you

"When you're in love, there's no need to understand what's happening, because everything happens inside you."

Learn to fly

"I'm not afraid of strong winds because I'm learning to fly."

Light Beneath the Wound

"Even the deepest wound holds a quiet lamp—those who stay long enough help it shine again."

One is Enough

"You don't need a hundred affirmations. You need one you're willing to live into every single day."

Our mind

"Our minds control us; we do not control our minds."

Path of Embers

"True paths begin not where you are comfortable—but where you were burned awake."

Peace

"To find peace, let go of your rage, lust, greed, guilt, and bitterness."

Peel away

"We must peel away the bitterness of life from time to time in order to reveal the richer aspects of life."

Responsibility

"In this life cycle, one must willingly carry out one's responsibilities by serving living beings while appreciating the beauty of life."

Sacred Stillness

"The soul doesn't always seek answers—it seeks a hand that doesn't flinch in the presence of pain."

Scent of Sincerity

"The universe doesn't respond to beautiful words—it listens for sincere frequency."

Small steps

"If you want to achieve greater things in your life, begin with small steps."

Softness is Strength

"In a world that hurries to harden you, staying soft is a quiet form of courage."

Stories We Swallow

"The most dangerous lies are the ones we tell ourselves and swallow whole—until we forget they were lies."

Storm's Gift

"The storm did not destroy him. It unwrapped the parts he'd hidden beneath safety."

Surrender Is Not Defeat

"Letting go is the bravest act of all; it's the conscious choice to trust that what is meant for you will find you."

The Blessed Burn

"What feels like punishment is often preparation in disguise."

The Calm Beyond the Storm

"Resistance is the tension before the release—when you surrender, the storm within settles and clarity emerges."

The Compass of the Soul

"Your emotional state is not just a feeling—it's a direction. It either leads you home or further from yourself."

The Door to Continuance

"Death is not the end but the moment the soul steps into its unspoken promise."

The Emotional Echo

"Unresolved emotions are like echoes in a valley—they keep returning until heard, felt, and freed."

The Eternity in a Breath

"All of time bows to one sacred truth: this breath, right now, is everything."

The Fire in Still Waters

"True courage is not loud—it burns steadily in the heart that keeps loving despite the storm."

The Furnace of Resistance

"The affirmations that cause discomfort are often the ones closest to your liberation."

The Gentle Liberation

"Letting go is not loss—it's the soul remembering how to fly without weight."

The Gentle Warrior

"Kindness is not weakness. It is the strength to remain open when pain would rather close you."

The Gift of Nothing

"When all is taken from you, and you still breathe peace—you have found the gift of nothing."

The Language of the Soul

"Silence isn't emptiness—it's the native tongue of the soul waiting to be heard."

The Lens of the Heart

"You don't see life as it is. You see life as your emotions paint it in that sacred, unseen moment."

The Light Beneath Ashes

"Hope does not shout—it glows, quietly, beneath the ruins of what once was."

The Patience Within the Seed

"Desire must be planted like a seed—not to be chased, but nurtured, trusted, and given time to bloom."

The Quiet Revolution

"Gratitude is the art of transforming the ordinary into the holy."

The Refuge of Ruin

"I found more refuge in the ruins than I ever did in the safety I tried to preserve."

The Return to What Is

"Awakening isn't discovering something new—it's recognising what's been calling all along."

The Sculptor's Hand

"Mastery is not control over marble, but stillness of hand when thunder surrounds you."

The Sculptor's Mind

"You are both the sculptor and the clay. What you repeatedly think, you eventually become."

The Sculptor's Silence

"A storm outside cannot shatter your creation—unless you invite the storm within."

The Song of Scars

"Your scars don't hide your story—they sing it back to the sky with tenderness."

The Space Between Breaths

"Real connection happens not in conversation, but in the space between the breaths we take beside each other."

The Strength to See

"To truly see another is the beginning of healing both yourself and the world."

The Thought Farmer

"Each thought you think is a seed cast into the soil of the soul. Tend to it with love, or risk harvesting what you never intended."

The Tuning Fork Within

"You cannot receive the song of joy while humming the tune of fear. Life echoes the pitch of your presence."

The Uncarved Path

"When what you built is taken, the path you never dared to walk becomes visible."

The Unseen Offering

"Even a broken prayer reaches God when it is honest."

The Unseen Offering

"You may think you did nothing—but the space you held changed something invisible forever."

Touched by Flame

"It wasn't the fire that changed me—it was what I discovered standing amidst the ashes."

True happiness

"The man who has broken the chain of pain and suffering finds true happiness."

Unseen Sculptor

"What the fire destroyed, the unseen sculptor replaced—not with form, but with meaning."

Want to be happy

"If you want to be happy, let go of your anger and bitterness and embrace kindness, compassion, faith, and love."

Wheel of Becoming

"Every collapse is a chance to reshape with deeper grace."

Whispers of the Wheel

"The wheel of transformation turns in silence—until one day, you become the vessel you were always meant to be."

Witness Over Fixing

"To witness suffering without trying to erase it is one of the rarest forms of love."

True Love

Spreading Compassion and Love

"To spread love and compassion is to light a candle in the heart, and by the warm glow of that candle, we can illuminate the deepest recesses of humanity."

- Shree Shambav

A moment

"Just celebrate and dance. Life is a moment we are living right now."

Anger

"Expand and increase your love to the point that fury can't touch it."

Appealing

"You are appealing because you are distinct."

Compassion

"When you are compassionate to others' needs, pain and suffering, misery and grief, and seek to alleviate them, you are living the ultimate truth."

Compassion is a Language

"You don't have to speak the same pain to understand it. Compassion speaks fluently across wounds."

Deepest love

"A woman with the deepest love is the one who wears a deep mask hidden behind a veil."

Dispel darkness

"The only thing that can dispel darkness is light. The only thing that can drive away hatred is love."

Echo

"The world, like a mountain, echoes your words back to you. Be in love no matter where you are or what you do."

Entire universe

"You are not alone; the entire universe is within you."

Essence

"Love is eternal; the aspect may change as the essence remains."

Eternal love

"We are immersed in eternal love and bliss when the soul merges in the supreme."

Falling in Love with Truth

"A true affirmation isn't meant to convince you. It's meant to help you fall back in love with your truth."

Flame of Remembering

"Even the smallest flame can remind a grieving heart that it still knows how to love."

From Thankfulness to Transformation

"Gratitude doesn't just change what you see; it changes who you are at the core."

Gratitude

The Heart's True Magnet: "What you appreciate expands—gratitude is the invisible force that pulls blessings closer."

Hearts Left Open

"We came close with questions. We left open with wonder."

Just like a candle

"A teacher is just like a candle, providing hope, direction, and light in life while nourishing the souls of individual students for a lifetime. All the time and effort invested in bringing out the best in children can never be repaid in mere words."

Kinder heart

"The smile on a child's face is the most priceless thing in the world. Never let the child inside of you die, and look after it whenever it needs something. You would improve everything if you had a kinder heart."

Longing

"Yearning for someone to love me."

Loss Is Not the End

"The ones we love may leave the world, but their essence remains—in how we walk, speak, and choose to live."

Love

"We are chasing love all over the place, but wait, it's right within us."

Love and compassion

"Intellect tangles and knots people, but love and compassion dissolve all tangles."

Love and kindness

"Love and kindness serve as a bridge between you and all living things."

Love begets love

"Love begets love; hatred begets hatred, forgiveness and love shall be exonerated besides being loved more."

Love in the Silence

"Before you conclude that no one has ever loved you, remember this: Somewhere, in a quiet corner of time, someone has wept silently for your pain, whispered prayers for your peace, and sacrificed pieces of their own happiness for your well-being. Love is not always loud—it often lives in the unseen, the unspoken, and the unforgotten."

Love, Unnamed and Shared

"Love, when not forced into language, becomes something holy."

Love's Unfinished Song

"Love never truly ends. It simply changes its language—from presence to memory, from voice to silence."

Never ages

"Man, deeply in love with nature, never ages."

Our minds

"Thirst drove me to the lake, and I drank the moon through my cupped hands because everything mirrors our thoughts. Isn't it true that our minds can alter everything?"

Pets

"In a short amount of time. It spends its time waiting for us, bringing us joy and laughter. They adore us regardless of our physical appearance or ability, whether we are wealthy or impoverished, decent or despicable. It makes no difference who we are."

Reflection

"What you ruminate on is attracted to your life. But you also attract into your life what you determine or judge. If you believe people are dishonest, you will attract dishonest people; if you believe people are bad, you will attract bad people. When you are worried about illness or disease, you attract more of it. Everything you think about becomes your cage and your reality. See empathy, abundance, peace, kindness, and honesty in all. You will be surrounded by beautiful things and healthy people."

Rooted in Love

"Like the Banyan, be the one whose roots touch many hearts even as you appear still."

Search

"Why are you looking outside when it is already inside you?"

Silence

"Anyone who does not comprehend your silence is unlikely to comprehend what you say or think."

Stillness is Strength

"In the silence after an affirmation, listen to your body. It will tell you whether it believes you."

Teachers

"With gratitude, I recall the excellent teachers. The learning is wonderful, and it can never be taken away, and I am grateful to those who have touched my human emotions."

The Abundance of a Grateful Soul

"When your heart overflows with thanks, the universe responds with endless abundance."

The Companion Called Grief

"Grief is not the enemy of love—it is its most faithful companion, still knocking at your door when the world forgets."

The Gift of Gentle Eyes

"To look upon someone's pain with soft eyes is a form of grace the world desperately needs."

The Home That Calls You Back

"All seeking ends in love—not as romance, but as the returning to where you began."

The Invisible Thread

"Even when loved ones depart the world, the thread between hearts is never severed—it becomes spiritual."

The Marriage, Not the Magic

"Affirmation is not magic—it is marriage: a lifelong vow to show up for who you are becoming."

The Warmth of Being Seen

"Being truly seen by another is a form of medicine no pharmacy can offer."

The darkest times

"Who comes into your life during the darkest times? Walk you back to the light."

The religion of Love

"You can be certain that the religion of love accepts everyone."

True concern

"You don't need to be brilliant, wealthy, attractive, or perfect to make a difference in someone's life. Just show some genuine concern."

True friend

"A genuine friend is a link to a life based on common values and principles. A connection to the past and a path to the future."

True love

"Radha and Krishna never met; they were always within each other."

Two-edged sword

"Excessive love and magnificent accomplishment are two-edged swords."

Where Love Lingers

"Healing begins not when the wound is gone, but when love decides to linger near it."

True Wisdom

Timeless Insights for Life

"Life's most precious moments are often silent epiphanies that gift us with timeless insights, guiding our steps and whispering the secrets of the universe to our souls."

- *Shree Shambav*

True Wisdom

A Thought Rewritten

"Your story isn't finished. And your next thought is the pen."

A candle

"Being a candle is difficult because one must first burn in order to emit light."

A change

"It's never too late to ask yourself: Am I willing to change from within?"

Ashes of Becoming

"When everything you clung to burns away, what remains is who you truly are."

Belief is Architecture

"What you believe becomes the scaffolding of your life. Weak beliefs build fragile futures."

Believe in yourself

"While many people take steps in doubt, their journey ends in no time. Those who struggle with faith will triumph in joy. Believe in yourself because you are capable of miracles."

Beneath the Effort

"Sometimes the greatest shift isn't doing more—it's aligning more with who you already are."

Better ways

"A progressive element is about learning and shifting to better ways and means of developing knowledge to heal oneself. 'We change our lives by changing ourselves.'"

Between the Breaths

"In the sacred space between inhaling sorrow and exhaling surrender, we remember who we truly are."

Bondage

"The mind is the source of bondage and liberation."

Born from the Breaking

"We are not ruined by our breaking—we are born through it, reshaped by grace into a deeper kind of wholeness."

Challenge

"Many times, we are challenged or driven out, not because we are not worthy of it, but because we are worth more."

Clean Space, Clear Mind

"Detoxifying your environment is the first step to detoxifying your life."

Companionship

"Who we are is determined by the company we keep."

Compassion

"I discovered true religion through empathy, compassion, love, and kindness. It requires belief in humanity's unity and a commitment to living these values together."

Comprehend

"Whoever does not comprehend your silence likely will not comprehend what you say."

Darkness

"Come out of the dark and enter the light."

Deep within

"Look deep within. You will find everything you seek."

Democracy in the Shadows

"The greatest threat to democracy is not the sword, but the slow suffocation of justice—delayed by silence, distorted by power, denied to the voiceless, and divided to maintain control. When truth is twisted and equality withheld, democracy doesn't collapse in chaos—it crumbles in neglect."

Don't be blind

"If you are critical about the flaws of others, then make sure you are not blind to your own."

Don't be depressed

"Don't be depressed about a 'misfortune,' because it could be a 'fortune.'"

Effort Without Clarity is Noise

"Not all motion is momentum. Not all striving is sacred. Sometimes, stillness moves more than effort."

Emotional Echoes

"Your thoughts don't end in your mind. They echo into your choices, your relationships, your breath—your becoming."

Empathy

"Empathy is all about finding sublime echoes of other people in yourself. Kindness begins with comprehending the suffering and grief around you. A wonderful gesture can reach a wound that can only be relieved by compassion."

Focus

"We can't simultaneously think of two things."

From Self to Service

"True manifestation blossoms when your desires serve not only you but the greater good."

Future's Ingredient List

"Your future doesn't ask what you wish for—it asks what you are feeding it daily in thought, emotion, and belief."

Growth

"Just as there is no end to learning, there is no end to growth."

Guard Your Gateway

"What you allow into your mind shapes the reality you create—choose your influences wisely."

Happiness and suffering

"Misery and happiness continue to appear in our lives, just as seasons on this earth."

Higher values

"When you focus on higher values, you cannot focus on lower thoughts or emotions."

Highest wisdom

"Knowing thyself is the highest wisdom."

Inner Climate

"Your dominant thoughts are the sun and rain of your inner world. They set the climate where your destiny grows."

Invisible seed

"A gigantic tree begins with an invisible seed."

Just keep moving

"As long as you keep moving, it doesn't matter how slowly you go."

Knowledge

"A thing that you possess truly cannot leave you."

Leave the shore

"You cannot cross the ocean without leaving the shore."

Let Go, Let Flow

"What you try to carry alone becomes heavy. What you place into trust begins to move on its own."

Letting Go to Receive

"When your hands are full of the past, you cannot hold the present."

Living the Law

"Manifestation is not just what you do—it is who you become."

Love as Manifestation's Highest Language

"When you give love freely, you open the floodgates for the universe to return it in abundance."

Magnetism in Motion

"When your soul's mission aligns with your daily actions, you become an unstoppable force of attraction."

Mastering oneself

"Knowing oneself is a sign of true wisdom; knowing others is a sign of intelligence. While exerting control over others is a sign of strength, true power is demonstrated by self-mastery."

Mind creates

"I'm frail; I'm heartbroken; I'm a moron; they have deceived me. The mind creates ridiculous doubts and quandaries about itself."

Persistence Lights the Path

"When passion fuels persistence, even the longest journey becomes a series of small victories."

Potter's Wisdom

"Like clay, we are shaped not in comfort but in the press of surrender and stillness."

Power of the mind

"It is better to elevate yourself through the power of your mind than to lower yourself because the mind can be both a friend and an enemy to the self."

Quest

"The quest of one man is the quest of all mankind."

Reflect

"The mind is liberated by reflecting on oneself."

Sagacity

"Transforming our tribulations into lessons swings into sagacity."

Secret

"A secret is like a bird. When it leaves our hand, it flies with its wings."

Seek knowledge

"Don't stretch your hands for alms; instead, outstretch them for seeking knowledge."

Silent Agreements

"Most limitations are not real—they are silent agreements we made with fear."

Small step

"Every journey begins with a single small step."

Starving the Shadows

"When you stop feeding your fears, they begin to starve. When you start feeding your faith, it begins to rise."

The Emptying

"Loss is not the absence of love, but the clearing of space for something greater to grow."

The Fire Within

"The fire that consumes your world may be the one that forges your soul."

The Invisible Threads

"You are always manifesting—not through effort, but through frequency. Check what you're vibrating."

The Kindness Loop

"Self-compassion is not indulgence—it's emotional recalibration. A return to centre."

The Mental Menu

"You wouldn't feed your body poison—why feed your mind self-doubt, worry, and regret?"

The Mirror of Belief

"Life reflects not what you want, but who you believe you are."

The Pause Between

"Wisdom lives in the pause between reaction and response. That pause is your power."

The Quiet Power of Patience

"Patience is not the absence of action but the presence of faith in the unseen rhythm of life."

The Ripple of Kindness

"Small acts of positivity spread wider than you imagine, shaping a world you wish to live in."

The Ripple of Presence

"Your authentic light draws others to their own power; being yourself is the greatest service you can offer."

The Sacred Pause

"Not every silence is empty. Some pauses hold the wisdom you were too busy to hear."

The Thought Apothecary

"Your thoughts are potions—some heal, some poison. Your awareness is the apothecary. Choose wisely."

Those in need

"Help the young in need. Later, they grow up to be productive achievers in life."

Time is the Alchemist

"The waiting transforms what you desire into what you deserve, refining your soul as it shapes your reality."

True happiness

"We constantly place value on the material world and consider it to be the source of ultimate truth and happiness."

True meaning

"You will understand the true meaning of a friend in time of need."

True taste

"When you are truly thirsty, you can taste actual water; when you are starving, you can taste actual food."

"Every time you think, you write a line in the script of your life. Speak to yourself as if the universe is listening—because it is."

Why?

"Why travel around the world when you already have everything you need in your vicinity?"

Your Vibe Attracts Your Tribe

"The energy you surround yourself with either fuels your dreams or dims your light."

View and Perspective

Cultivating Inner Peace

"In the heart's stillness, we find the sanctuary of inner peace, a place where life's storms may rage outside, but tranquillity reigns within."

- Shree Shambav

View and Perspective

Act, Not to Impress—but to Express

"True purpose never seeks applause—it simply flows, fully expressed and unafraid."

Blossom always

"Be as delicate as a flower at all times. A flower can still bloom when surrounded by thorns, but you can't smile if you're in pain."

Change

"What you see is influenced not only by what you look at. But also, by where you look. The things you look at change as you change your perspective on them."

Dancing flower

"In ecstasy, a dancing flower. 'They are delicate yet firm, soft yet withstand strong winds. Their certainty and desire to live indefinitely. Isn't this incredible - just a moment's existence and such faith in eternity?'"

Excess

"A delicious meal needs pepper and salt, but if they dominate, the meal is ruined."

Forest Within

"You may not save the forest, but you can keep the forest alive within your choices."

From Thought to Thread

"Every joyful action is a golden thread, stitching the unseen fabric of your future."

In the Quiet, We Return

"What the world calls breaking is often the beginning of becoming—of returning, unmasked, to who we truly are."

Invisible Invitations

"Sometimes purpose hides in ordinary moments—waiting to be seen through quiet joy."

Joy as Compass

"The lightness in your heart is not a distraction—it is direction."

Nature's message

"Nature's message was always present, just waiting for us to notice it and open our hearts and minds like butterfly wings. Ascend to newer levels of elegance and beauty. There is always beauty at the end of every painful experience."

Nescient

"Earth's nescient ground awaits metamorphism. Nature's head and guide in those steps shall be Truth."

Perfect friend

"One who seeks a perfect friend will find none."

Perspective

"We gain perspective when we step back and look at things from a distance, which allows us to appreciate their worth. Everything we hear is an opinion, not a factual statement. Everything we see results from our perspective, not reality. We can change our truth if we change our perspective."

Purpose Is a Frequency

"When you move in joy, you don't chase your destiny—you call it closer."

Real self

"When you pass judgment on others, you define your real self."

Sacred Doesn't Always Shout

"The divine rarely arrives in noise—it slips in, quietly, through what feels true."

Sincerity Is Scale

"The weight of your action lies not in how far it reaches, but in how true it feels."

Stagnant

"Hate is like stagnant water; love is like a free-flowing stream; never be stagnant since it causes physical, mental, and emotional suffering."

Stillness Is a Decision

"Stillness is not inactivity. It's the deepest form of clarity before the sacred move."

The Art of Remembering

"The soul never truly forgets where it came from—it only waits for silence deep enough to hear the way back home."

The Bird That Never Left

"You were never broken—only taught to forget you could fly."

The Bridge of Breath

"Every breath you take in stillness is a bridge to everything."

The Crownless Throne

"Only those who kneel to truth rise with grace."

The Door Unlocked

"Forgiveness isn't forgetting—it's freeing yourself from a prison built by pain."

The Fire and the Feather

"Even in the blaze, a single feathered soul can carry water if moved by love."

The Frequency of Forward

"When you act from love instead of lack, the universe doesn't just respond—it aligns."

The Gentle Revolt

"Truth doesn't scream—it whispers until the noise gives way."

The Gentle Yes

"Not every truth arrives with thunder. Some come wrapped in stillness, waiting for your quiet yes."

The Great Uncaging

"When you dissolve into all things, you finally find your Self."

The Guiding Flame

"The quiet voice within you is not small—it's the compass of stars wrapped in a whisper."

The Inner Compass

"When the step feels like peace, not panic—that's when you know it's aligned."

The Light Within the Delay

"Procrastination is not always laziness—it is often a sacred pause, asking if your next step is truly yours."

The Moment Unmeasured

"Joy doesn't require reasons—it lives where presence and surrender meet."

The Offering Unseen

"Every unseen act of kindness becomes a thread in the soul's tapestry."

The Sacred Unfolding

"What you let go doesn't vanish—it transforms into the wings you've been waiting for."

The Seed's Patience

"No seed curses its slowness—it trusts the rhythm of becoming."

The Silent Sculptor

"Time doesn't pass—it shapes, carves, and teaches in invisible strokes."

The Soft Power

"Bend like the tree, not because you are weak—but because you know how to rise again."

The Unveiling of Meaning

"In losing what we clung to, we remember what can never be taken."

The Wildflower in Ruin

"Hope grows in the cracks of what we thought was over."

The beauty of silence

"Plants and flowers taught me that happiness comes from within and that one can nourish oneself in silence."

Troubled water

"Never let your thoughts become troubled water, as it is difficult to see through murky water. Instead, be like a fresh running stream, and your answer will get cleared."

Understand mortal nature

"Where is the time for all the trivial things in the chaos and mayhem if you are aware of your mortal nature?"

Wheel of life

"Things reverted to the old cycle seems 'slow and dry,' always."

Where it goes

"The wind blows wherever it pleases, and you can hear it, but do not know where it comes from or where it goes."

Whispers That Move Mountains

"Your soul doesn't shout—it whispers. And if you're still enough, even the quietest nudge becomes a revolution."

Whispers of Purpose

"True purpose rarely shouts—it often arrives as a gentle nudge dressed in stillness."

Wings Are Not Always Feathers

"Freedom is not the absence of pain, but the presence of courage to rise while carrying it."

You Are the Flame, Not the Smoke

"In the storm of urgency, remember: you are not the chaos—you are the calm fire that shapes it."

Life is Priceless

A flower blooms in the quietness,

Beside the pond beneath the tree,

On the plains and along the green lanes,

On the ridges and along the edges.

They continue to shine like a star,

Waving and dancing in glee,

Giggling and whispering with flies and butterflies,

Like they've known each other for aeons.

Flowers dancing in ecstasy,

Are delicate but strong,

Soft but fight against strong winds,

They are fleeting but self-assured.

Try to communicate with the flower,

By simply approaching it,

Keep your stillness, open your ears,

To hear the euphoria of flowers.

Listen, You'll find out for sure.

Not only does she dance in ecstasy,

She sends messages in the wind,

A nostalgic whisper to the one she loves.

A whisper of love spreads its fragrance.

Happiness spreads all around.

Isn't it amazing? She looks beautiful,

Because she makes others appear beautiful.

LIFE CHANGING JOURNEY

Have you encountered flowers?

Worried, restless, or insecure,

They believe they will live eternally,

Isn't that incredible? Only a moment exists,

But such a conviction in eternity.

Your life is like a priceless flower,

You cannot live it in pain and in vain,

You are not a burden on this earthly plane.

Dancing like an ecstatic flower, light and strong,

Live a glorious life, leaving a mark of memories.

- Shree Shambav

Life Coach and Philanthropist

Shree Shambav is the visionary founder of the Shree Shambav Ayur Rakshita Foundation (www.shambav-ayurrakshita.org). He founded this institution with a lofty goal: to recognise human identity across gender, ethnicity, and nationality. Through this organisation, he wants to assist all communities in realising their full potential and the intrinsic beauty of life.

Shree Shambav, a Life Coach, is dedicated to supporting people on their journeys of self-discovery and empowerment. He assists people in discovering who they are, determining what inspires and drives them, and overcoming limiting ideas. His approach clarifies what one wants in life, assisting people through goal-setting and a step-by-step process for achieving them. He empowers people to make deliberate and responsible decisions, allowing them to identify their blind spots and evolve as individuals via the use of numerous strategies and tools.

The foundation's bold, uncompromising, and compassionate ventures are always aimed at initiating the "Inner Transformation" process. They focus on spiritual growth, personal growth, and self-healing while emphasising that true progress lies in "Inclusive Growth and Co-existence." This philosophy drives all their initiatives, encouraging a holistic approach to development and well-being.

Under Shree Shambav's leadership, the foundation has launched several impactful movements:

Shree Shambav Green Movement: This mission is to create a healthy, green, and clean earth through responsible water conservation and greening initiatives. The movement strives to make the world a green paradise by encouraging sustainable living and environmental responsibility.

Shree Shambav Vidya Vedhika (Vizhuthugal): This project aims to help students and children by offering training, books, stationery, and uniforms. It aims to provide the next generation with the tools and resources they need to excel both academically and personally.

Shree Shambav and his foundation exemplify the spirit of compassion, transformation, and inclusive growth via their work, which has a profound impact on individuals and communities around the world. His work exemplifies the power of acknowledging and nourishing the human spirit, creating a world in which everyone can reach their full potential and appreciate the beauty of life.

TESTIMONIALS

Journey of Soul - Karma - "We die in our twenties and are buried at eighty." Remember that nothing can stop someone who refuses to be stopped. "Most people do not fail; they simply give up." Shree Shambav deserves full credit. It allowed me to sit and consider what I might miss out on in life. The author has delved into every aspect of our daily lives. How can a seemingly insignificant change in these seemingly insignificant details bring us such joy? The Soul of Journey teaches you the "art of living" as well as the "art of dying."

Twenty + One Series - The rich cultural heritage offered a host of twenty + one short stories with incredible imagination, morals and values prevalent at a given time, influencing how people respond to a crisis or any situation. The author has recreated images with universal values and morals. The plentiful of fascinating from faraway lands would leave the modern play and story writers a cringe. The book supports trust and immeasurable values, instilling hope for the new generations.

Death - "Shree Shambav's 'Death - Light of Life and the Shadow of Death' is an extraordinary masterpiece that delves deep into the profound questions surrounding our existence and mortality. The book's opening statement, 'Nothing ever truly dies; it simply ceases to exist in one form before resuming it in another,' sets the stage for a thought-provoking exploration of death's multifaceted nature. Shambav's remarkable ability to navigate the philosophical complexities of death and our universal fear of it is both enlightening and comforting. This book is a testament to the power of understanding and acceptance."

Whispers of Eternity - "Reading 'Whispers of Eternity' by Shree Shambav was a transformative experience that left me captivated from beginning to end. Each section of this exquisite collection delves into the myriad facets of existence, offering poignant reflections on life, death, and everything in between. Shree Shambav's verses are a testament to the beauty of language and the power of expression, inviting readers to embark on a journey of self-discovery and spiritual awakening. Whether celebrating life's simple joys or grappling with the complexities of human emotion, this book is a timeless companion that speaks to the heart and soul of every reader."

Life Changing Journey Series - "Life Changing Journey Series II Inspirational Quotes" is a remarkable collection that illuminates the path to self-discovery and personal growth. With its inspiring quotes and insightful reflections, this book serves as a beacon of light in a world often shrouded in darkness. Each quote offers wisdom, guidance, and encouragement, reminding readers of their inner strength and resilience. A must-read for anyone seeking inspiration and enlightenment.

Learn To Love Yourself – "A Heartfelt Guide to Authentic Self-Love." "Learn to Love Yourself" invites readers on a transformative journey to embrace their true essence in a world often focused on external validation. Through ten insightful chapters, it gently reveals principles of genuine self-love, guiding readers to deepen their connection with themselves. Beyond surface positivity, it encourages the cultivation of resilient self-acceptance, from embracing one's unique qualities to setting empowering boundaries. With inspiring stories and practical wisdom, this book is a trusted companion on the path to inner peace, fulfilment, and joy, helping readers build lives that reflect their authentic selves.

The Power of Letting Go – This book has been a gift to my spiritual journey. Shree Shambav's insights into attachment, personal growth cycles, and forgiveness are enlightening. The concept of seven-year cycles resonated with me, helping me understand the natural phases of life. I feel more empowered to let go of what no longer serves me and step into a life of freedom and fulfilment. A truly beautiful read!

A Journey of Lasting Peace – "A Journey of Lasting Peace" feels like a trusted friend guiding you through the maze of self-discovery. The 18 transformative principles are both practical and deeply resonant, addressing everything from gratitude practices to the art of letting go. Each chapter is infused with warmth and wisdom, making it easy to apply the concepts to my life. I particularly appreciated the emphasis on physical health's connection to mental well-being; it served as a wake-up call for me to prioritise my health. This book is an invaluable resource for anyone serious about personal growth!

Astrology Unveiled Series – "Profound, Logical, and Inspiring". What stands out in Astrology Unveiled is the author's dedication to making Vedic astrology logical and approachable. Each concept flows naturally into the next, backed by examples and exercises. The insights into karma and life cycles add a philosophical depth rarely seen in astrology books. Perfect for anyone seeking spiritual growth alongside astrological knowledge!

The Entitlement Trap - "Thought-Provoking and Challenging" The book challenges readers to confront their own sense of entitlement, and that's not easy—but it's essential. The Entitlement Trap doesn't offer a one-size-fits-all approach. Instead, it's a thoughtful, layered examination of how entitlement can limit our growth. The chapter on "Defining Your Own Hill" was particularly impactful, as it pushed me to reconsider which challenges are truly worth pursuing. A thought-provoking read for those willing to do the inner work to create a life they can be proud of.

Whispers of a Dying Soul – "A Soul-Stirring Reflection on Life's Unspoken Truths" - *Whispers of a Dying Soul: Unspoken Regrets and Unlived Dreams"* is a deeply moving exploration of the unexpressed emotions and unfulfilled aspirations that shape our lives in ways we often don't realise. This book invites readers to confront the powerful, often hidden impact of regret while guiding them through a journey of introspection and healing. Each page opens a space to reflect on the choices that define us—from moments of unspoken love to neglected passions—offering a gentle reminder to live authentically and courageously.

Whispers of the Soul: A Journey Through Haiku - is a mesmerising collection that speaks directly to the heart. Each haiku is a delicate brushstroke capturing life's fleeting beauty and timeless wisdom, inviting readers into moments of deep reflection and peace. This book is a balm for the soul, guiding us to find meaning in stillness and connection in simplicity. The themes of nature, love, and mindfulness echo universal truths, resonating with quiet, powerful grace. It's a book to be savoured slowly, cherished deeply, and returned to often. Truly, it is a gift for anyone seeking calm and clarity in life's chaos.

Whispers of Silence - Unlocking Inner Power through Stillness by Shree Shambav is a rare gem that beckons readers to pause, reflect, and reconnect with their inner selves. In a world that never stops talking, this book offers a profound exploration of silence—not as a void but as a rich and transformative space.

From the first page, Shree Shambav's writing resonates deeply, blending scientific insights with spiritual wisdom in a way that feels both universal and deeply personal. The author's ability to bridge the tangible and the transcendent makes this book an invaluable guide for anyone navigating the chaos of modern life.

The Power of Words: Transforming Speech, Transforming Lives - The Power of Words is a profound and enlightening guide that has transformed the way I approach communication. Shree Shambav masterfully uncovers the hidden influence of our words on relationships, self-perception, and overall well-being. This book doesn't just teach you how to speak; it inspires mindful communication that fosters connection and trust. The insights on replacing negative patterns like gossip and judgment with kindness and authenticity are truly life-changing. The practical strategies and engaging narratives make it an invaluable resource for personal and professional growth. A must-read for anyone striving to communicate with intention, clarity, and compassion. Highly recommended!

The Art of Intentional Living: Minimalism for a Life of Purpose - "The Art of Intentional Living is a refreshing guide to finding clarity in a cluttered world. With practical wisdom and profound insights, it inspires you to simplify, prioritise, and live with purpose. A must-read for anyone seeking balance and fulfilment."

Awakening the Infinite: The Power of Consciousness in Transforming Life - "Awakening the Infinite is a transformative guide that expands the mind and nourishes the soul. With profound insights and practical wisdom, this book beautifully explores the power of consciousness, helping readers connect with their true purpose and inner potential. It is a journey of self-discovery, healing, and spiritual awakening, offering clarity and inspiration at every turn. A must-read for anyone looking to live with greater awareness, meaning, and authenticity."

Beyond the Veil: A Journey Through Life After Death:

"This book touched me in ways few others have—it's not just about death, but about life, meaning, and the vast unknown that connects them. Beyond the Veil offers a graceful blend of science and spirit, inviting us to explore the mystery with awe rather than fear. The stories, insights, and reflections linger in your heart long after the final page. A truly transformative read that brings light on the shadows of mortality. It reminded me that in embracing death, we truly learn how to live."

Bonds Beyond Blood:

"A profoundly moving story that reminds us family is not defined by blood, but by love, sacrifice, and the courage to heal. Every chapter touched my soul with its emotional truth and timeless wisdom. Through joy, grief, and redemption, this book captures the raw beauty of human connection. I saw reflections of my own family in its pages—both the pain and the hope. A powerful, unforgettable read that lingers long after the final word."

A Journey into Spiritual Maturity: 12 Golden Rules for Inner Transformation

"This book is a gentle yet powerful guide that awakened a deeper sense of purpose within me. Each golden rule felt like a mirror reflecting truths I needed to embrace. Shree Shambav's wisdom is timeless, poetic, and profoundly grounding. It's not just a read—it's a journey into the heart of who you truly are. A must-read for anyone seeking lasting peace, clarity, and inner transformation."

The Inner Battlefield: Overcoming the Enemies of the Mind and Soul:

"This book is a powerful revelation—an honest mirror to the battles we fight within. Every chapter is a step closer to clarity, peace, and emotional mastery. Shree Shambav brilliantly transforms ancient wisdom into practical guidance for modern souls. It awakened in me a new strength to face my fears and rise above inner turmoil. A must-read for anyone seeking true inner victory and lasting transformation."

The Seeker's Gold – Unlocking Life's Greatest Treasure

The Seeker's Gold is a soul-stirring masterpiece that goes far beyond the pursuit of wealth—it is a journey into the heart of what truly matters. Each chapter unfolds with poetic wisdom and emotional depth, revealing that life's real treasure is not found in riches but in the transformation of the self. As the protagonist evolves through trials, love, and profound realisations, so does the reader. This book is a mirror for every dreamer, a lantern for every seeker, and a companion for anyone walking the path of purpose. A timeless tale that stays with you long after the final page.

ACKNOWLEDGEMENTS

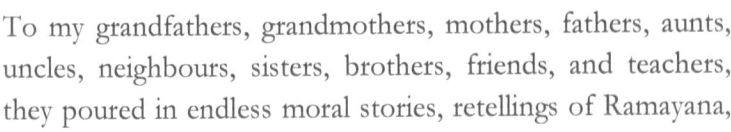

To my grandfathers, grandmothers, mothers, fathers, aunts, uncles, neighbours, sisters, brothers, friends, and teachers, they poured in endless moral stories, retellings of Ramayana, Mahabharata, Puranas, Upanishads, and so on.

My teachers, neighbours, and kindred souls. Who provided us with a stage to perform wonderful Puranic stories and were gracious enough to acknowledge our efforts.

The artists and translators of epics have served as a source of inspiration, invigorating our spirits, making these works accessible, and enabling us to grasp the profound depths and deeper dimensions they contain.

I also cherish the stimulating conversations I had with my wonderful mothers, Punitha Muniswamy and Uma Devi.

Our family's youngest member, Aadhya, who always overwhelmed me with questions, inspired this book.

I would likewise prefer to express gratitude to Mr Sivakumar, Mrs Roopa Sivakumar, Mr Akshaya Rajesh, Ms Akshatha Rajesh, Ms Apeksha Prabhu, Mr Akanksh Prabhu, Mr Nikash Sarasambi, and Mrs Spoorthi Nikash for their valuable inputs.

I must thank Mr Rajesh, Mr Savan Prabhu, Mrs Revathi Rajesh, Mrs Rajani Sarasambi, and Mrs Manju Reshma, who encouraged me and often suggested writing a book. Their unwavering belief that I had something valuable to offer kept me going during my writing sessions.

Love you all,

Shree Shambav

www.shambav.org

shreeshambav@gmail.com

www.ingramcontent.com/pod-product-compliance
Lightning Source LLC
LaVergne TN
LVHW091540070526
838199LV00002B/139